HOLLYWOOD *Snapshots*

The Forgotten Interviews

Michael B. Druxman

Published in the USA by:
BearManor Media
P O Box 71426
Albany, Georgia 31708
www.bearmanormedia.com

Printed in the United States of America
ISBN 978-1-62933-146-1 (paperback)

Book & cover design and layout by Darlene Swanson • www.van-garde.com

Other Books by Michael B. Druxman

Fiction

Murder in Babylon

Dracula Meets Jack the Ripper & Other Revisionist Histories

Once Upon A Time In Hollywood: From the Secret Files of Harry Pennypacker

Shadow Watcher

Nobody Drowns In Mineral Lake

Non-Fiction

Miss Dinah Shore

Life, Liberty & The Pursuit of Hollywood

My Forty-Five Years In Hollywood And How I Escaped Alive

Family Secret (with Warren Hull)

The Art of Storytelling

The Musical: From Broadway To Hollywood

One Good Film Deserves Another

Charlton Heston

Merv

Make It Again, Sam

Basil Rathbone: His Life and His Films

Paul Muni: His Life And His Films

Stage Plays *(The Hollywood Legends)*

Ava & Her Guys

The Last Monsters

Robinson & Raft

Lana & Johnny Were Lovers

Sexy Rexy

B Movie

Clara Bow

Chevalier

Flynn

Gable

Jolson

Lombard

Nelson and Jeanette

Rathbone

Tracy

Orson Welles

Other Stage Plays

Hail on the Chief!

Putz

The Summer Folk

Screenplays

The Amusement

Barry & The Bimbo

Black Watch / The Cavern

Charla

Cheyenne Warrior

Cheyenne Warrior II / Hawk

Dillinger & Capone

Ghoul City

Matricide

Ride Along

Sarah Golden Hair

The Summer Folk

Uncle Louie

In Memory of

The Hollywood That Was

Contents

Introduction

During my tenure in Hollywood, I was fortunate enough to meet and work with many actors, directors, producers, writers and other great artists who created the classic movies that we still revere today. In several instances, these talented individuals became personal friends.

While I was working as a publicist for these clients, I was also writing books and, later, stage plays about Hollywood's "Golden Era" and the people who populated it. I wrote seven non-fiction books in the 1970s and early 80s.

They are all now out-of-print, though two of them (i.e. *Basil Rathbone: His Life and His Films* and *Paul Muni: His Life and His Films*) have been revised in recent years and are, once again, available.

Additionally, during this period, I was engaged to write a monthly column for *Coronet Magazine,* "Yesterday at the Movies." Each column was devoted to a legendary actor or actress who was a part of Hollywood's "Golden Years."

Coronet, sadly, ceased publication decades ago.

Sometime in the mid-1980s, I began writing my series of stage plays about Clark Gable, Carole Lombard, Errol Flynn, Al Jolson and other great stars, collectively titled, *The Hollywood Legends.* At this writing, there are sixteen plays in the series, many of which have had multiple productions throughout the United States. Two of them, *Orson Welles* and *Clara Bow,* have been recorded on audio and are available for download. All are available in paperback and Kindle editions.

Recently, while digging through my storage space, I came across my original, virtually forgotten, interview notes for almost all of my books and several of my stage plays. I perused them and realized that many of the fascinating things that these people said to me never wound up in my finished books, magazine articles or plays.

Certainly that's not an uncommon occurrence for a writer. You might chat with a subject for hours and get a lot of interesting stories out of him or her, but when you sit down to write your book, magazine article or play, you pick and choose the material that fits into your narrative.

For the most part, I didn't even use what these people said to me in my two memoirs.[1] Indeed, in those books, I usually only discussed my general encounters with the artists, not what they *said* to me when I did the interviews.

My work on this book is more organization than actual writing. My purpose is to preserve the anecdotes, memories and opinions that these wonderful subjects related to me in the interviews.

The first section, "Yesterday at the Movies," was the easiest to do. I, simply, included my original column from *Coronet*, followed by quotes from the subject that I discovered in my interview notes that weren't included in the published article.

Keep in mind when reading these columns that they are snapshots in time. They were all written during the 1970s, and they represent what the interviewee knew or said at that particular moment. Subsequent events may have made some of their statements inaccurate.

The rest of the book is more scattershot. They are quotes from interviews I conducted for my various books and stage plays. Since they do not have a magazine piece to anchor them, I've utilized footnotes, whenever necessary, in an attempt to put these random quotes into context.

I hope you will enjoy this trip down memory lane.

---

1 *My Forty-Five Years in Hollywood… And How I Escaped Alive* (2010) and *Life, Liberty & The Pursuit of Hollywood* (2013), both published by BearManor Media.

Yesterday at the Movies

Jack Oakie

Jack Oakie

Happy Birthday to You, Jack Oakie

The afternoon I spent with Jack Oakie was more of an experience than an interview.

*Oakie and his wife, former actress Victoria Horne (*The Scarlet Claw, Harvey*), were good friends of my editor, Doris Bacon and her husband, columnist James Bacon. She suggested that I interview the actor and set an appointment for me to visit his home on a Saturday afternoon.*

What I didn't know at the time and, in fact, didn't learn until recently is that, for most of his life, Oakie was "functionally deaf." Throughout his career, he performed primarily with the aid of lip reading or vibrations.

As I reported in my memoir, My Forty-Five Years in Hollywood ... And How I Escaped Alive*:*

Mrs. Oakie greeted me at the door of the mansion that used to belong to Barbara Stanwyck and ushered me into the family room. A few minutes later, Jack strolled into the room, pretended not to see me, and then treated me to one of his triple takes.

We chatted for a few minutes, and then he offered me a drink. I opted for a diet soda. Jack poured a full fifth of vodka into a large beaker for himself and, over the next hour, proceeded to down the whole thing.

During that time, he told me some great show biz stories. Then, since this was before the coming of VHS and Beta, he brought out his16mm movie projector and screen, and showed me a half-hour reel of clips from many of his movies.

There was definitely some hilarious stuff on that reel, but I didn't need Jack, who was by then feeling pretty good, to point out every funny bit to me. No kidding, after every clip, he'd turn to me and shout, "Wasn't that funny, Mike? Wasn't that the funniest thing you ever saw?"

The next day, Vickie Oakie phoned me and asked me not to write that Jack had been drunk during the interview. I assured her that I was only interested in his anecdotes.

The column ran in the November 1973, issue of Coronet.

"I didn't think I'd ever get a job in the movies," reflected Jack Oakie in a recent interview.

"When I first came to Hollywood, everybody was dark and swarthy. Me, I had red hair and freckles."

The robust actor/comedian/vaudevillian had arrived in Southern California via the S.S. President Hayes on a June morning in 1927. He decided to make the journey from New York on the advice of the father of comedienne Pert Kelton, who owned a hotel in Los Angeles and had offered Jack a free room until he began working.

"I'd recently been fired out of the chorus of a Rodgers and Hart show, *Peggy Ann*, and no other jobs were in sight. Lindbergh had just flown the Atlantic. So, I figured if he could take a chance, so could I."

Two days after Jack hit Hollywood, he went to a party where he met director Wesley Ruggles. The following day, Ruggles signed him to a personal contract and gave him a small role in *Finders Keepers* starring Laura LaPlante. He was on his way.

The master of the "double-take" (He calls his version "a triple with a fade.") turns 70 on November 12th. During his varied career, Oakie has starred in one hundred motion pictures: *Tin Pan Alley, The Great Dictator, Wintertime, Call of the Wild, Million Dollar Legs, Rise and Shine, The Eagle and the Hawk, Once in a Lifetime, If I Had a Million* and *Hello, Frisco, Hello* being among the most popular.

The red hair has turned white now and the round face contains a few wrinkles. But, aside from that, it was still the same energetic Jack Oakie who greeted this writer when he visited the performer's ten-acre estate in Northridge, California, last July. The alert and cheerful entertainer with the twinkle in his eye ... and cheeks ... is still going strong. He enjoys meeting new people and, of course, reminiscing about the show business of yesterday.

"You know," he said, as he pulled his chair closer, "I'm the only actor to get his song encored in a movie theater.

"I made a film in 1929 called *Sweetie,* in which I sang a song, 'Alma Mammy,' doing an Al Jolson impersonation. At the premiere, the audience applauded so loudly that the projectionist stopped the picture, ran the film back and showed that number again."

Jack Oakie was born Lewis D. Offield in Sedalia, Missouri, but was raised in Muskogee, Oklahoma: "Mother was a professor. Father was a grain dealer and a minister.

"When I first got into show business, people said I sounded like I was from Oklahoma, so I adopted the name 'Oakie.'"

He recalled his first meeting with Charles Chaplin: "Everybody knew that Chaplin was preparing a film about Hitler. So, when he sent for me, I figured he wanted me for the role of Goering. When he told me he wanted me to play Mussolini, I wasn't sure I was Italian enough for the part.

"'Jack,' he said, 'what's so funny about an Italian playing Mussolini?'

"He was right and I told him right then that I'd do *The Great Dictator.*"

One of Jack's early films was with character actor Ned Sparks who, as Jack puts it, "kept fish-eyeing me in our scenes together." ["Fish-eyeing" is a show business term for a performer who upstages his fellow players by continually staring at them without expression.]

After a few hours of Sparks' trick, Jack was very upset and complained to director Wesley Ruggles. "Jack," inquired Ruggles, "where are your hands?"

Jack Oakie was never upstaged again.

Oakie worked with most of Hollywood's greatest stars, and on each of them he bestowed his own personal nickname: Clark Gable was "The Moose," Alice Faye was "Faysie," Betty Grable became "Bee Gee," Chaplin was "The Boss," Spencer Tracy was affectionately dubbed "The Street Singer" and Bing Crosby, of course, was "The Groaner."

Offers keep coming in regularly for Oakie to appear in various films or on television. Most of them are refused. "The rewards are not great enough in show business today," said Jack. "Everybody wants you to appear for scale. Why should I appear on a show with a host, who gets thousands of dollars a week, and get nothing for it?"

Oakie has always felt strongly about performers getting a fair wage. Members of the Screen Extras Guild, who worked on pictures with him back in the 1930s and 1940s, remember fondly that Jack would often deliberately "forget" his lines just so the extras could earn overtime.

Jack Oakie: actor, entertainer and a great guy.

AND HE ALSO SAID:

"When I was fifteen, I had a summer job as a telephone clerk on the New York Stock Exchange."

"On my first film, the cameraman told me 'Don't ever put make-up on.'"

"The stage manager of *Peggy Ann* didn't like me because, as a chorus boy, I was doing 'too much'. Then, I wore my tuxedo costume to a party and he fired me."

"We shot *Call of the Wild* on Mt. Baker in Washington State. I drank brandy to keep warm. Gable wrestled with the dog... and Loretta Young."

"When we were doing *The Great Dictator,* Chaplin said to me 'We know when we're funny.'"

AFTERWORD:

Jack Oakie died on January 23, 1978, in Los Angeles, California at the age of 74 from an aortic aneurysm.

Claire Trevor

Claire Trevor

You Can't Get An "A" Without A Fight

Claire Trevor was the second interview I did for my Coronet *column.*

Previously, I'd spoken to her on the phone about her participation in the original Stagecoach, *a chapter in my the book I was preparing on movie remakes,* Make It Again, Sam.

I drove down to Newport Beach from my then-home in Agoura Hills on the night before the interview, spent the night in a motel, then drove up to her hilltop home the next day to do the interview.

Miss Trevor and her husband, Milton Bren, were perfect hosts, treating me like an old friend. We spent two or three hours chatting and I was sorry when the afternoon ended.

Several years later, when Bren passed away, I sent Miss Trevor a letter of condolence and, shortly thereafter I received a letter that Bren had written, apparently in anticipation of his death.

I know I still have the letter someplace, though I have no idea where it might be (a problem that one faces often as one gets older). However, I've never forgotten one thing he said in that letter that Miss Trevor had sent to everyone who had expressed their sympathies. Paraphrasing:

"I would like to come back to Earth for one day, shake the hand of everybody I ever met, and thank them for giving me such a wonderful life."

This interview with Claire Trevor appeared in the January 1974 issue of Coronet.

Humphrey Bogart, Hollywood's number one tough guy, was desperate. He had to get Claire Trevor that role in *Key Largo*. Her husband was shaming him into it.

Miss Trevor, the proud owner of both an Oscar and an Emmy, sat in the living room of her Newport Beach home last August and reflected on how she captured the role that earned her the Academy Award.

"I read the script and thought I'd be right for 'Gaye,' the former singer who'd become Eddie Robinson's alcoholic girl friend. I really wanted that role.

"Unfortunately, the bosses at Warner Brothers didn't want to pay me my regular salary, as they figured that one of their contract players could be had for less.

"Then, my husband, Milton (Bren), took over. He knew that our friend Bogie wanted me for the part and decided to work on him."

Bren, a writer/producer, was in a steam room with Bogart when he started to needle the actor. "You're no big star," he began. "If you had any influence with Jack Warner, you'd insist that Claire play the part."

Bren saw that the movies' Sam Spade was on the defensive, so he continued his attack: "If you had any guts, you'd pick up that phone right now and tell Warner that, if Claire doesn't do the film, neither will you."

After an hour of this abuse, Bogart called the studio head and delivered the message. Later that afternoon, Claire Trevor, "Queen of the 'B' Pictures," had been cast in *Key Largo*.

"It was the first time that I'd ever gone after an important role," said the actress, "and it paid off."

Her real name was Claire Wemlinger. Her first agent didn't like it, so he picked the Trevor moniker out of a New York phone book.

Claire came to Hollywood from the Broadway stage in 1933 as a contract player for Fox Pictures. Her first film was *Life in the Raw*, a "B" western starring George O'Brien.

"I fell madly in love with George," she recalled, "and thought he was one of the most charming men I'd ever met. When he told me he was about to get married, I was crushed."

Claire did twenty-two "B" pictures between 1933 and 1937, none of which are worth remembering except for the casts. Her co-stars included Spencer Tracy, Lew Ayres, Brian Donlevy, Cesar Romero, Gilbert Roland and James Dunn.

Darryl Zanuck, who'd taken over the studio reins when it became 20th Century-Fox, was not very impressed with the actresses' star potential and was satisfied to let her stay in low budget pictures, which were making money. Besides, he liked to discover his own *major* stars, not inherit them from another regime.

"I could never push myself," Claire said. "It was my own non-fighting nature that kept me from going after the really important roles. Also, I rationalized that I was only in Hollywood temporarily and would soon go back to Broadway for a show."

Claire compounded her situation by refusing to cooperate with the studio publicity department, as she felt that going after press was too "pushy." "In those days," she recalled, "every actress had a label. I didn't want to be known as 'The Ear' or 'The Toe.'"

William Wyler, working through Goldwyn Studios, was preparing his film adaptation of the popular stage play, *Dead End*. He sent for Claire. "At last," she thought, "I'll get to work for a great director."

Wyler's first remark to the actress was: "Tell me, Miss Trevor, what have you done?"

"I was destroyed," she remembered. "I know I was no Garbo, but I had starred in twenty-two "B" pictures. Wyler hadn't seen any of them and was just interviewing me at Sam Goldwyn's suggestion. Then, when he offered me a role that was only two pages long in the script, I was really hurt."

But Claire looked over the part and realized that she could make this short scene effective enough so that Hollywood would finally notice her. The role was 'Francie', a prostitute and ex-girl friend of gangster Humphrey Bogart. The actress gave a brilliant performance and earned an Oscar nomination.

"Today, if that had happened," said Claire, "I would be rushed into one 'A' picture after another. But, Zanuck couldn't have cared less that I was nominated. He sent me back to the 'Bs'."

She got another chance to work with a top director when John Ford gave her star billing in a picture called *Stagecoach*. It was, of course, a huge success, but did little to further Claire's career.

"When the film was released," she said, "my agent went out of town for six months and nobody was around to pursue better roles for me."

On the other hand, *Stagecoach* won Thomas Mitchell an Oscar and made a star out of a previously unknown actor, John Wayne.

Claire continued to work regularly in Hollywood because the producers respected her talent. However, as she was not an *important* star (ala Joan Crawford or Bette Davis), she was still doing leads in the low budget projects and supporting roles in the "A" films. Her better pictures in the 1940s include: *Dark Command* with John Wayne, *Texas* with William Holden and Glenn Ford, *Honky Tonk* with Clark Gable (she remembers him as "a big teddy bear"), *The Adventures of Martin Eden* with Glenn Ford and *Murder, My Sweet* with Dick Powell.

In 1948, *Key Largo* changed everything. The picture was directed by John Huston and had an impressive cast – Bogart, Robinson, Lauren Bacall and Lionel Barrymore. Yet, when Claire did her "big" scene, in which Robinson made her beg for a drink by singing "Moanin' Low," audiences forgot about the other players and watched only her.

She won the Oscar and, at last, Claire Trevor was an *important* name.

The roles and the pictures got better through the years. She continued to work steadily, winning an Emmy for the television production of *Dodsworth* and another Academy Award nomination for her performance in *The High and the Mighty*.

Today, however, she enjoys staying home, painting and enjoying the company of her husband, children and grandchildren.

Will she work again? "Of course, I will," Claire replied. "But, only if a *good* part comes along."

Claire Trevor: a beautiful, intelligent, gracious lady. She's achieved most of her goals in life, including the important one: happiness.

AND SHE ALSO SAID:

"I hate the hours of doing theatre. I hate going to work when others are going home."

"I wore crumby clothes in *Dead End.* I was used to having costumes made for me. I didn't comb my hair; wore old make-up. I felt like a dirty orphan.

"I didn't want anybody to see me. I wanted to look my best all the time."

"If you're in this business and want to succeed, you must promote yourself."

"I didn't want to go see John Ford when he asked to see me for *Stagecoach.* I had fever blisters on my face from the sun. It was swollen.

"I went to the set and held a hanky over my face the whole time."

❧

"I didn't think that *Key Largo* was that good.
I'd seen the play and didn't like it.

"But, it was a happy cast. Very relaxed. John Huston took his time, which drove Jack Warner crazy.

"Harry Lewis, who played the 'kid killer,' wound up owning the Hamburger Hamlet restraurants."

❧

"I advised Grace Kelly to go home and quit. Acting is a rough life.

❧

"She was a fan of mine, but later she snubbed me."

❧

"I'm a good cook when I get going."

❧

"I got jobs from talent, not name value."

❧

"I wanted to do *The African Queen, The Yearling, A Streetcar Named Desire* and *None But the Lonely Heart."*

❧

"I think I'm happier than all the stars I know."

AFTERWORD:

Claire Trevor died of a respiratory illness in Newport Beach, California, on April 8, 2000. She was ninety years old.

Her husband, Milton Bren, had passed away in 1979.

Mary Pickford

Mary Pickford

"America's Sweetheart"

As I recall, it was my editor's suggestion to interview Mary Pickford for my Coronet *column.*

*I liked the idea, but I was also skeptical that the silent film star would be interested in making herself available for an interview. After all, she had been out of the public eye for many years, living with husband Charles "Buddy" Rogers (*Wings*) in her legendary "Pickfair" in Beverly Hills.*

Apparently, Doris Bacon, my editor, knew Rogers. She made a phone call which resulted in my being able to do a lengthy phone interview with Miss Pickford, the result of which appeared in the April, 1974, issue of Coronet.

I'm not one hundred percent sure, but I believe that I was the next to last person to interview Mary Pickford. The last person was a writer for the Los Angeles Times, who interviewed her in connection with special award she was given in 1976 by the Motion Picture Academy.

Sidebar Stories: Several years before all this took place, I was driving in the tangled hills of Beverly Hills and I got lost. I had a meeting with a possible client, whose name I don't recall.

I came across an open gate to a long driveway and, thinking this might be the place, I drove up to this remarkable estate. I parked my car, knocked on the door and asked the butler who answered, "Is this the home of so-and-so?"

"No, sir," he replied. "This is Pickfair."

I'm sure that my mouth dropped open with a "Wow!"

The butler was kind enough to give me directions to where I was going, and I left.

In the mid 1980s, when I was writing my one-woman play, Clara Bow, *I got to visit Pickfair officially. Actually, it was the back part of the estate.*

After Miss Pickford's death, her widower, Charles "Buddy" Rogers, had sold the main house and built himself an impressive new home on the property. He had worked with Clara Bow in Wings, *the first film to win the Best Picture Oscar, and I went there to interview him. I have a poster from that silent classic, signed to me by Rogers, hanging on my wall.*

"I told Mr. D.W. Griffith that if he wanted me to work for him, he'd have to double my salary," recalled Mary Pickford in a recent interview.

The then unknown actress had been filming for the director for only one day (the going rate was five dollars), when she decided that she wanted more money. "I had a big job on my hands," she continued. "I had to make money for my mother, brother and sister. Besides, I was a Belasco actress and, for that reason alone, I was entitled to the raise."

Griffith, later the director of *The Birth of a Nation,* was impressed with the spunky fifteen-year-old girl and, as per her request, increased her salary to ten dollars.

Mary Pickford, "America's Sweetheart," was the screen's first star. Indeed, she was probably the most popular female personality in the history of the art form.

Born Gladys Smith in Toronto, Canada, she began working in stock companies at the age of four. Then, when she was thirteen, she cornered the noted stage producer, David Belasco, who cast her in his production of *The Warrens of Virginia.*

Eventually adopting her grandfather's surname, Mary went to work for Griffith at Biograph Studios in 1909. Her first starring role was in *The Violin Maker of Cremona* with Owen Moore, who was to become her first husband.

In those early days of the cinema, players did not receive screen billing, as producers felt that unknown actors would work for less money. However, following her first major hit, *The Little Teacher* (1909), audiences and exhibitors began to refer to Miss Pickford as "Little Mary," "Goldielocks," The Girl With the Curls" or "The Biograph Girl."

Finally, after being recognized by two people on a subway, she went to Griffith and again demanded a raise. "The director inquired, "Are you a better actress today than you were yesterday?"

"No," she replied, "but if my privacy is going to be taken from me, I want more money." She got the raise.

It was not long before Mary had a reputation within the motion picture industry of being a very astute businesswoman: "I never took advantage of the fact that I was good at business. I just knew what I was worth and went after it."

1912 found Mary back on the New York stage, working for David Belasco again in *A Good Little Devil.* The theater was constantly mobbed, since it was the first time in history that film fans had seen one of their idols in person.

Following her departure from Biograph in 1913, she went to work for Adolph Zukor at Famous Players, starting at a salary of five hundred dollars per week. For that motion picture pioneer, Mary made such films as *Tess of the Storm Country, The Girl From Yesterday, The Foundling* and, later, *Captain Kidd, Jr.*.

"I owe 'Papa' Zukor a great deal," said Mary. "It was his idea that I continue to dress in socks and a bow, and play little girls. In fact, the greatest thrill of my career was when I found out that I could do that kind of part convincingly."

By 1916, the actress had signed a deal with Zukor, which guaranteed her one million dollars within a two year period, plus bonuses.

Mary Pickford did two films for Cecil B. DeMille in 1917, *The Little American* with Jack Holt and *Romance of the Redwoods,* which she considered her "biggest flop."

Mary didn't enjoy working for C.B.: "He put on too many airs and graces.

Whenever Mr. DeMille walked on the set, his assistant would blow a whistle, then he would stride in, dressed in his riding boots, and give a whole performance.

"Griffith was a much greater director. He invented more in one day than DeMille did in his entire lifetime."

In order to produce their own films, Charles Chaplin, Griffith, Mary, and her second husband, Douglas Fairbanks, Sr., formed United Artists in 1919. The company's initial offering was *Pollyanna,* the first film ever sold to exhibitors on a percentage basis. Other Pickford pictures, like *Suds, Little Lord Fauntleroy* (she played a dual role in this, her favorite film), and *Sparrows,* followed.

Mary recalled that she didn't like *Sparrows* when it was first made, but in recent years, she has grown quite fond of it. "It was a hard picture to do," she said. "I felt a tremendous responsibility to the children who were in it with me and I made sure that, since we were working in mud up to our shoulders, they always had warm blankets and hot cocoa after they finished a shot."

After winning the 1929 Oscar for *Coquette,* Miss Pickford made her only movie with Fairbanks, an early talkie version of *The Taming of the Shrew.* Of her performance in that disaster, she commented: "I have no qualms about admitting that Katherine was one of my worst performances. Instead of being a forceful tiger-cat, I was a spitting little kitten."

Miss Pickford recalls her 1933 release, *Secrets,* with Leslie Howard: "I walked off that stage after my last scene and an 'inner voice' said to me, 'This is goodbye, Mary.' And that was it. I never worked again in pictures."

In 1953, she sold her interest in United Artists and, since then, she has been virtually inactive professionally. She now lives with her third husband, the charming and "good-looking" Charles "Buddy" Rogers, who she first met when they co-starred together in *My Best Girl* (1927) and married after she divorced Fairbanks in 1935. The couple resides at her legendary Beverly Hills estate, "Pickfair," from where she has reined since Hollywood's Golden Era.

Although Mary Pickford was, probably, the most successful actress in motion picture history, her biggest disappointment stemmed from the fact that all the films in which she played an adult role were failures: "I felt that

I was an actress and that I didn't have to play little girls all the time. But, the audiences wouldn't accept me as a grown-up. They're the boss, you know."

AND SHE ALSO SAID:

"Mother gave me my business sense. She said, 'Never take less.'"

"I was a great admirer of Charlie Chaplin.
I thought politics were beneath him.

"Charlie never answered the telephone. He hated them."

"I made more money for producers
than I made for myself."

"Leslie Howard was a great actor, but miscast in *Secrets*. He was too gentle... refined. The part should have been played by Clark Gable."

"Our films belong to the public. They should never be destroyed."

AFTERWORD:

Mary Pickford died of complications from a cerebral hemorrhage in Santa Monica, California on May 29, 1979. She was eighty-seven years old.

Paul Henreid

Paul Henreid

Two Cigarettes and a Lot of Suave

I first met Paul Henreid at a Christmas Party held at the Beverly Hills home of one of my publicity clients, director Edward Dmytryk.

My then-wife, who had had a couple of drinks and was feeling good, spotted him across the room filled with celebrities (e.g. Sean Connery, Betty Garrett, Larry Parks), strolled over and took his arm. "I've been in love with you ever since I was a teenager," she said.

"Thank you," Henreid replied, beaming his captivating smile. "I'm very flattered."

We introduced ourselves, had an amiable chat and, for the moment, that was that.

A couple of years later, I was researching Make It Again, Sam, *my book on movie remakes, and I phoned Henreid to discuss his participation in the 1962 remake of the Rudolph Valentino silent classic,* The Four Horseman of the Apocalypse.

Surprisingly, he remembered me.

"The two leads" (Glenn Ford and Ingrid Thulin), he told me about the film, "were both good actors, but were wrong for the parts. They were not emotional or gay enough. Events that seemed unavoidable in the first version seemed studied and planned in the remake."

A few months later, after I started writing for Coronet, *Henreid seemed like a perfect subject for my column, which appeared in the May, 1974 issue.*

"We all thought *Casablanca* was going to be a tremendous flop," recalled Paul Henreid in a recent interview at the Beverly Hills Brown Derby restaurant. The suave Austrian actor had, of course, starred with Humphrey Bogart and Ingrid Bergman in the now immortal Warner Brothers picture.

"They were constantly re-writing the script while we were shooting," he continued. "Every couple of days, we'd get a new scene or two to film. I asked the director, Michael Curtiz, how he felt about the way the movie was progressing and he confessed, 'I have no idea what we're doing. I'm just shooting the pages they give me.'

"It's a miracle the picture turned out as well as it did."

Although he was born in Trieste, Italy, Henreid grew up in Vienna, where he eventually became a steadily working stage and film actor. 1928 found him playing a secondary role in *Only a Comedian,* a film starring the great German actor, Emil Jannings.

In the story, Paul had been killed and was lying in a coffin. Jannings insisted that Henreid actually get into the closed casket, even though he would not be seen by the audience, as it would aid him (Jannings) in "feeling" the scene better. Since he considered it an honor to work with the character star, the young man obliged.

He lay there for a half-hour, assuming that the scene was in the process of being shot. Finally, becoming a bit curious, he peered out to find that the cast and crew had all gone to lunch.

Eventually, Henreid traveled to London where, following a stage appearance as "Albert" in *Victoria Regina,* he was hired for a major part in Metro-Goldwyn-Mayer's *Goodbye, Mr. Chips* starring Robert Donat and Greer Garson. It was his first English-language film.

Hitler had taken Austria and there were fears that he would soon be in England. Realizing that as an Austrian subject the Fuhrer could have him shot as a traitor, Paul accepted an offer to do a play, *Jersey Lily,* on Broadway and departed for America. Upon his arrival, he learned that the production had been cancelled.

His performance in another play, *Flight to the West,* attracted the attention of Hollywood. Initially signing with RKO for one picture per year, he was soon over at Warner Brothers to star with Bette Davis in *Now, Voyager,* in which he introduced his well-known romantic "trademark" of lighting two cigarettes simultaneously.

The bit was Henried's idea in the first place. He'd suggested it to replace some cumbersome business written into the script. But director Irving Rapper wasn't convinced. So, the actor went to Bette Davis, who agreed with him. They, in turn, enlisted the aid of Hal Wallis. The executive producer spoke to Rapper and the idea of two cigarettes was adopted.

Reflected Henried: "My wife and I had actually been lighting cigarettes this way for years. The practice stemmed from the fact that in those days cars didn't have cigarette lighters, so when I was driving and wanted to smoke, my wife would light my cigarette for me in that manner."

Based on the success of *Now, Voyager,* Warner Brothers made Henried a very lucrative offer to sign with them on an exclusive basis. The deal was so good that he couldn't turn it down. At that studio, his credits were impressive: *In Our Time* with Ida Lupino; *Between Two Worlds* with John Garfield; *Devotion* starring Lupino and Olivia deHavilland; *Deception* with Bette Davis; and a remake of *Of Human Bondage* with Eleanor Parker inheriting the Bette Davis role.

Paul recalled that the preview of the latter picture was a disaster: "I was there with my agent, Lew Wasserman, who is now head of Universal Pictures. We sat up until four in the morning, trying to decide how the movie could be re-edited.

"The next day, I gave Lew two pages of notes I'd written, suggesting alternate ways to cut the film. He memorized the list, then visited the producer of the picture, Henry Blanke, who was also depressed and baffled as to how to fix the thing.

"Lew started making suggestions. Blanke was so impressed that he called in his secretary and had her take notes. Ultimately, he utilized all except two of my suggestions in the finished film.

"It's funny, but to this day, Blanke doesn't know that those ideas came from me and not my agent."

As the years went by, Henreid acquired a strong desire to work behind the camera: "I was getting very annoyed at the directors I was working with, so I decided to do something about it."

Also, Warners was not giving him any exceptional roles and were refusing to loan him to other studios, which were offering such plums as *Gaslight* and *Anna and the King of Siam.* He did work at Metro-Goldwyn-Mayer in that studio's *Song of Love* with Katharine Hepburn, but he otherwise found his position quite frustrating.

In 1948, he produced and starred in a suspense thriller, entitled *Hollow Triumph,* taking over the directorial reins about halfway through the filming schedule. Three years later, he received his first directing credit in an exposé of college fraternities, *For Men Only.* Coincidentally, his most impressive film as a director was *Dead Ringer,* made in 1963 back at Warner Brothers with his good friend and former co-star, Bette Davis.

Henreid was a conspirator in one of Hollywood's classic pranks. John Barrymore, a close friend of Errol Flynn, had died. Humphrey Bogart and Peter Lorre came to Paul with the idea to borrow the actor's corpse from the funeral parlor, then leave it sitting in a chair at Flynn's home. Henreid went along with the gag at first, but when it came to handling a dead body, he "chickened out."

The joke still worked, however, and when Errol Flynn walked into his house that night, he received the shock of his life.

Today, Paul Henreid prefers to work only when the situation is right. He no longer likes to direct or act on television, feeling that the fees are inadequate compensation for the time involved. Recently, he completed a road tour of Shaw's *Don Juan in Hell* and there is a possibility of his co-starring in a major feature, based on a Hemmingway novel, later this year.

In person, he is very much like his screen image, a gentle, sophisticated and very nice man.

AND HE ALSO SAID:

"When I first read the script for *Casablanca,* it was nothing like it eventually turned out to be. In fact, I considered it a melodrama of very little significance.

"Hal Wallis, the producer, is the real hero of *Casablanca.* He saw that it was an average melodrama, yet he wanted to make it a better one. Out of his determination came a picture that we didn't know we had."

"Greer Garson was 'jittery' when we made *Goodbye, Mr. Chips.* She didn't understand what Sam Wood, the director, wanted. Robert Donat and I worked with her, so that she'd feel more comfortable."

"I loved working with Bette Davis. She's a perfectionist and more intelligent than many people you work with."

"After *Now, Voyager,* Warner Brothers offered me a seven-year term deal, but I turned it down. I wanted to freelance.

"Then, the United States entered the war and aliens, like myself, had problems. I figured that if a major studio had me under contract, they would protect me, which is why I changed my mind and signed the contract."

AFTERWORD:

The Hemmingway picture that Henreid had hoped to do, *Across the River and Into the Trees,* did not happen.

He died of pneumonia in Santa Monica, California on March 29, 1992. He was eighty-four years old.

Ann Miller

Ann Miller

Still Lovely to Look At

I did not jump with joy when Doris Bacon, my editor at Coronet, *asked me to interview Ann Miller. Yes, she was a terrific hoofer and a marvelous comedienne, but there were many other stars of Hollywood's Golden Era who I would have much preferred to interview for my monthly column.*

Miller happened to be a personal friend of Doris, so I made a deal with her. I'd do a column on Ann if I would be allowed to do a future column on Howard Keel, who was then a publicity client of mine. She agreed.

I arrived at Miller's Beverly Hills home mid-afternoon, as she was just finishing up a meeting with renowned choreographer Hermes Pan, a very pleasant gentleman. Unfortunately, Miss Miller was not as affable. She struck me as being extremely cold, and we seemed to have an instant dislike toward each other.

"I don't know why you need to interview me," she said. "Why don't you just read my autobiography?"

Once Pan departed and I explained to her that I wanted to write my own piece, she settled down and we had a satisfying talk.

The interview appeared in the June 1974 issue of Coronet.

Anticipating your double take when you read it, remember that this was several years before the revolution in Iran.

Harpo Marx scared me to death," reflected Ann Miller in an interview earlier this year at the Beverly Hills home she'd owned since 1942.

She was referring to a 1938 film she'd done with The Marx Brothers and Lucille Ball at RKO, *Room Service*: "The first time I came on the sound stage, Harpo chased me around the set, wearing only his top hat and shorts and honking his horn. I was only about fourteen at the time and he really shook me up. He must have liked the way I screamed because, from then on, he chased me every time he saw me."

"And, if that wasn't bad enough, Groucho was always making funny cracks about my legs."

Born in Houston, Texas, the raven-haired dancer's father was a noted criminal attorney, who had defended such infamous clients as Bonnie and Clyde and Pretty Boy Floyd. In fact, Ann recalled, at the age of four, she accompanied he father on a prison visit to see client Floyd and wound-up being bounced on the gangster's knee.

After her parents were divorced, she moved with her mother to Los Angeles, where she took dancing lessons and, eventually, began working in club engagements. "I was only eleven," Ann admitted, "but I lied about my age so that the bookers would hire me."

Lucille Ball and comedian/talent scout Benny Rubin were attending a San Francisco premiere of one of the comedienne's films when they spotted the young hoofer working in a local nightclub. They were so impressed that they arranged for her to have an RKO screen test, which resulted in her being signed to a seven-year contract.

"My agent also represented dancer Eleanor Powell," Ann said, "but the studio bought me because my price was lower."

Miss Miller did well at that studio, appearing in such pictures as *Stage Door, Having Wonderful Time* and *Radio City Revels*. On loan-out to Columbia, she appeared with Jean Arthur and James Stewart in Frank Capra's classic, *You Can't Take It With You*. "I got fat on that movie," she remembered.

"Jimmy Stewart kept bringing me candy bars. He got skinny and I just put on weight."

She lost the excess poundage on her next job, when she went to New York to star in George White's *Scandals of 1939*. Her specialty number, the "Mexicongo," was a nightly showstopper and she returned to Hollywood to be paid a salary of $3000.00 per week, as opposed to the $150.00 she was getting when she left.

Back at RKO, she starred for George Abbott in *Too Many Girls*: "George wanted me to go back to Broadway with him and work there. He said that I could become the biggest musical star in show business. But, I wanted to stay in California where my home was."

Following a hitch at Columbia where she starred in a string of successful "B" musicals ("Whenever Rita Hayworth got out of line, they told her that I would take her place and she shaped-up."), Ann got the break she had been waiting for.

Over at MGM, Cyd Charisse had torn some tendons in her leg and the studio was looking for somebody to replace her in *Easter Parade* starring Fred Astaire and Judy Garland. Ann tested, got the part and a term contract. Now, audiences started to see her in good roles in top-budget musicals. Her credits at the studio included such hits as *On the Town* with Gene Kelly, *Hit the Deck, Kiss Me Kate* (her favorite film) and *Lovely to Look At.*

On the latter picture, Ann remembered that Red Skelton kept the cast, which included Howard Keel and Kathryn Grayson, constantly laughing: "Red was such a clown that all he had to do was look at us and we'd all break up. At one point, Louis B. Mayer came down to the set and wanted to know why the movie was three days behind schedule.

"We all pointed to Red."

With the demise of the Hollywood-style musical in the mid-1950s, Ann departed the Culver City studio to conquer other areas of the entertainment industry.

Today, she is often seen on television, as well as on the summer stock circuit. A few seasons back, she had a major success when she appeared on Broadway for a year in *Mame.* Her autobiography, *Miller's High Life,* was a big seller and video audiences can hardly forget her musical commercial for Great American Soups, the most expensive advertisement in television history ($250,000.00).

Very prominent on the Hollywood social scene, Ann is a close friend to the Iranian Royal Family, whom she met several years ago through dance director Hermes Pan.

"I got a movie offer from that part of the world once," she said. "A Lebanese producer had a role that had me dancing in a nightclub wearing gold paint... and nothing else. I quickly showed him the door."

AND SHE ALSO SAID:

"Frank Capra spoiled me when we did *You Can't Take It With You.* We sat around in a circle in chairs, going over the script before the cast got on its feet. He took the time to get every scene right.

"Of course I was a dancer, but I lied to Frank that I'd done toe work because I wanted the part. I didn't know that with toe work, you had to wrap your toes in lambs wool. I didn't do it. My toes bled and my feet were damaged beyond repair."

"I had the chance to do *Best Foot Forward, The Pajama Game* and *By Jupiter* on Broadway, but I wanted to stay in California."

"I gave Gene Autry his first screen kiss in *Melody Ranch.* He was very manly, much married, but he liked to look."

"Howard Keel may have had a great singing voice, but he couldn't dance. On *Kiss Me Kate,* we called him 'old tangle foot.' He kept stepping on his own feet.

"During the 'We Open in Venice' number, Katie Grayson got sick on the treadmill."

"Fred Astaire was very conscious of his height. I'm 5'7." He was only an inch or two taller. I had to wear ballet shoes in our dance numbers."

"My first husband pushed me down a flight of stairs while I was pregnant and broke my back and I had a miscarriage."

"The Look: When I left Metro ... The minute you don't have a contract or a job, people don't look you in the eye. They give you a wet handshake.

"There's a look of admiration or awe, a special look, when you are a success. Treasure that look and know you're a success, because when people don't give you that look, you're in trouble."

AFTERWORD:

Ann Miller passed away in Los Angeles from lung cancer on January 22, 2004. She was eighty years old.

Her last film was David Lynch's *Mulholland Drive.*

John Carradine

John Carradine

The Monster-Maker

I can't really say that I "knew" John Carradine, but we had many encounters over a period of twenty-five or thirty years.

He was an actor I always admired, and I found him to be a kind, gracious gentleman, yet I always felt that there was a sad quality about him.

The first time I encountered him was in the late 1950s in my hometown of Seattle. I was involved with the Cirque Playhouse, a local theatre group and Carradine was imported to star in two of its productions, The Winslow Boy *and* Shadow and Substance. *During rehearsals, he fascinated company members with his stories about the people he'd worked with in Hollywood.*

In the mid-sixties, after I'd moved to Los Angeles, I produced and directed a short film, Genesis, *and hired Carradine for three hundred dollars to narrate it, a task that took him about fifteen minutes to complete. However, he did hang around the recording studio and reminisce about old Hollywood for another twenty minutes, which was the best part of the afternoon.*

A few years later, after I had begun my publicity business, I represented a young actor, Bruce Carradine, but only after the elder Carradine phoned me to assure me that Bruce was, indeed, his adopted son. Awhile after that, I encountered Carradine on the set of The Astro Zombies, *a Ted V. Mikels "epic" that I'd been hired to publicize. He was, of course, playing a "mad scientist" in that one.*

In the early 1970s when I was researching my book, Basil Rathbone: His Life and His Films, *I drove up the California coast to Oxnard where I spent two or three hours interviewing Carradine in his seaside condo. Shortly after that, my editor agreed that he would be a good subject for my monthly column in* Coronet, *and that interview, which appeared in the July, 1974, issue of the magazine, took place on the set of* The Horror Hall of Fame, *an ABC television special, narrated by Vincent Price. I was a "creative consultant" on that special and, in fact, had suggested that Carradine be hired for the show since he was the last surviving member of the classic Hollywood horror film.*

That was, as I recall, the last time I saw Carradine. In 1988, I attended his funeral.

Incidentally, John Carradine, as well as Lon Chaney, Jr. and Bela Lugosi, is a principal character in my stage play, The Last Monsters, *available in both paperback and Kindle editions via Amazon.*

"I never played a monster," said veteran character actor John Carradine. "I just created them. In fact, I've played so many mad doctors that somebody should make me an Honorary Doctor of Spastic Pathology."

The gaunt, cadaverous-looking performer, who recently turned sixty-eight, was recalling his show business career, which has included roles in over two hundred motion pictures, including twenty-six horror films.

Indeed, the death of Lon Chaney, Jr. last year gave Carradine the dubious distinction of being the last of the great horror stars who frightened audiences during the 1930s and 40s. Pictures featuring Boris Karloff, Bela Lugosi, Chaney, Lionel Atwill and Carradine have become classics and still entertain, if not frighten, horror buffs of all ages.

Carradine entered the field of horror, in earnest, after he starred as a doctor who changes an ape into a beautiful girl in the 1943 epic, *Captive Wild Woman.* He later resurrected Lon Chaney Jr, in *The Mummy's Ghost,* then when Bela Lugosi wasn't available for the part, starred as filmdom's most famous vampire in both *House of Frasnkenstein* and *House of Dracula.* He recalled: "I told the producers that I would not play Dracula as a 'monster,' and said 'yes' to the role only after they agreed to let me make myself up like the character description in Bram Stoker's book."

It's a little known fact that Carradine was an early candidate to play Universal's Frankenstein's monster, the role that shot Boris Karloff to stardom. Reflected the actor: "I was called out to the studio for a test and, when I got there, I noted that the make-up man was mixing the ingredients to cast a 'death mask' of my face. I asked him what the part was that I was up for and he replied that they wanted me to play a monster. Then, when I was told that I would make no sounds, save an occasional grunt, I said 'No, thank you' and left. I never regretted that decision, but Boris, who took the role three months later, always did."

Carradine found it disturbing that he is best known for his work in horror films, rather than some of his more distinguished dramatic work. For years, he was a "charter member" of director John Ford's "stock company." The actor's performances in such Ford films as *Stagecoach, Mary of Scotland, Drums Along the Mohawk,* and, especially, *The Grapes of Wrath,* are unforgettable.

"Actually," reported Carradine, "Ford and I didn't get along at first. I'd been called in to test for the part of the sadistic guard in *The Prisoner of Shark Island* with Warner Baxter. 'Pappy' himself directed the test and, almost immediately, there seemed to be a personality clash between us. He wanted me to play the guard as a 'blithering idiot'. I didn't."

Later, one of the crew informed Carradine that Ford expected everyone to call him "Commander," to which the independent-minded actor retorted: "I'm not in the Navy!"

Carradine was surprised to learn that he'd gotten the role in Ford's picture, which turned out to be a hit and garnered the performer a contract at 20th Century-Fox. During his years at the studio, he appeared in such memorable films as: *Alexander's Ragtime Band, Ramona, Jesse James* and *The Return of Frank James* (as Bob Ford), *Blood and Sand, Swamp Water, The Black Swan* and *The*

Hound of the Baskervilles. The pictures he did on loan-out were also impressive: *Captains Courageous, Of Human Hearts* (as Lincoln), *Five Came Back, Hitler's Madman* (as Heydrich) and *The Adventures of Mark Twain* (as Bret Harte).

Carradine wanted very much to play the role of the minister in John Ford's *How Green Was My Valley,* but he lost the assignment to Walter Pidgeon: "If another actor beats me out of a part, I don't care, providing he's a good actor. But, if he's lousy, I get bitter about it. Pidgeon was magnificent in *Valley,* so it didn't bother me."

In his younger days, Carradine's idol was John Barrymore and the two became close friends. He'd met the legendary actor in 1930, the same year that he'd made his film debut (under the name "John Peter Richmond") in a sound remake of *Tol'able David.* Carradine got the job because his landlady was the director's mother-in-law and she figured that if she got her tenant the part, he'd be able to pay the back rent.

Carradine, who considered the job beneath him, didn't hit it off with this director either. During his first scene, the director called "Cut!" and said: "This isn't Shakespeare, you know."

Replied the actor: "Who the hell said it was?"

The performer recalled some valuable advice he once received from a director in New Orleans: "It was in 1925 and I was making my stage debut at the St. Charles Theater in *Camille.* We were in the middle of a rehearsal when I heard the director say, 'Young man, you are in love with your voice!' It was the most valuable criticism I ever received as an actor."

With three of his five sons doing well in the acting profession, it seems as if Carradine has started somewhat of a theatrical dynasty. David stars on television in *Kung Fu,* Keith is making a name for himself in features (*Emperor of the North Pole*), and the youngest boy, Robert, has a television series, *The Cowboys.* The Carradine name will, evidently, be on theater and television screens for many years to come.

Returning to the subject of horror movies, Carradine, whose first love is

Shakespeare, recalls the time when, during the filming of a vampire picture, he broke up the cast and crew by sitting up in his coffin, looking straight at the camera, and saying: "If I am alive, then why am I here? Yet, if I am dead, then why do I have to wee-wee?"

AND HE ALSO SAID:

"When I was a struggling young actor, I used to go up to the Hollywood Bowl late at night, get up on the stage and recite Shakespeare, projecting my voice as far as it would go. That is, until the police chased me out.

"Years later, I learned that it was John Ford who called the cops on me."

☙

"I did *The Proud Rebel* with Alan Ladd. He was so short and I was so tall that they dug a hole for me to stand in for our scenes together."

☙

In the train robbery scene from *Jesse James,* the local horses didn't work well, so we had to import 'movie horses' from Hollywood to Missouri.

☙

"I did the jump onto the train, not a stuntman. In fact, I did my own riding and running mounts for thirty years."

☙

"John Ford thought he had to create animosity with his actors. On *Mary of Scotland,* he called me 'a son-of-a-bitch'. Donald Crisp caught me before I hit him."

❧

"If John Ford saw two actors talking on the set, he'd want to know what was being said."

❧

"David (Carradine) doesn't work like me. He underplays. It's a good contrast. He did 'Laertes' to my 'Hamlet' years ago in stock."

❧

"The first scene in *Stagecoach* convinced me that John Wayne was star material. Wayne doesn't think he's an actor. All I ask of an actor is that I believe him."

❧

"I find it difficult to read lines and vomit at the same time."

AFTERWORD:
John Carradine died of natural causes on November 27, 1988 in Milan, Lombardy, Italy. He was eighty-two years old.

ANOTHER AFTERWORD:
As I was doing the final editing on this manuscript, I remembered a story about John Carradine, related to me many years ago by Howard Keel.

Keel and Carradine had once appeared together in a summer theater production of the Lerner-Lowe musical, *Camelot.* Howard knew the show quite well, having played "King Arthur" in several earlier stagings, but this was the first time that Carradine had been cast as the comical "Pellinore." A veteran dramatic character actor, Carradine was not known for playing comedy.

"During the second or third day of rehearsal," Keel recalled, "I could see that John was having problems 'finding his character,' so I approached him during a break and offered to give him some tips as to what I'd seen other actors do to bring 'Pellinore' to life.

"John looked at me like I was a gift from heaven. 'Oh, would you please, dear boy,' he said. 'I am totally lost, and anything would help.'

"John wound up 'stealing' almost every scene he was in."

Howard Keel

Howard Keel

Big Man With a Big Voice

Howard Keel was my publicity client for ten years and a friend until his death in 2004. Even after we ended our business relationship, I would see him fairly regularly, since he was a cast member on the Dallas *television series and Steve Kanaly, also a* Dallas *regular, was one of my clients.*

Howard was a client when I was writing my "Yesterday at the Movies" column for Coronet, *which is probably the reason my editor was reluctant to let me interview him for the publication. However, we made a deal. I agreed to interview her friend, Ann Miller, if she would let me do a Howard Keel column a couple of months later.*

This piece appeared in the August, 1974 issue.

"I spent my first eight months at MGM doing nothing," recalled Howard Keel, "and they were paying me $850 per week."

The tall, handsome baritone had been signed by the Culver City studio near the end of 1948 to star opposite Judy Garland in their proposed production of Irving Berlin's hit stage musical, *Annie Get Your Gun.*

He continued: "Although I'd been on Broadway, I'd only done one other movie, a low budget British film called *The Small Voice,* and was anxious to get more film experience before I started work on such an important project as *Annie.* But, Louis B. Mayer was firm. He insisted that I make my Hollywood debut in a musical. So, as Garland was busy on another picture, I just sat around and collected my pay."

The production of *Annie Get Your Gun* was plagued with troubles. On the second day of filming, the horse Keel was riding slipped and fell on him, which resulted in the actor breaking his ankle. He wore a walking cast for several weeks while the company shot around him.

Then, after some six weeks of shooting, Garland collapsed from "nervous exhaustion." Reflected Keel: " You could see that she just wasn't 'right'. She was 'gone'. I suppose she was on uppers and downers just to keep going."

Annie shut down for 3-4 months while the studio heads decided what to do. One of their first decisions was to replace director Busby Berkley with George Sidney, the problem having to do with a difference in artistic conception on the project. Shortly thereafter, Frank Morgan, who had been playing Buffalo Bill, died of a heart attack. Louis Calhern assumed his role.

Once it was realized that Garland would not be back, all of the previously filmed footage was scrapped and the picture began anew, this time with Betty Hutton in the lead. From that point, production proceeded relatively smoothly.

When *Annie Get Your Gun* premiered in April of 1950, critics raved about Keel's performance, the *Los Angeles Times* calling him "a Gable who sings." The actor was on his way.

Instead of putting their new male star into another important feature, the studio assigned him to appear with swimming star Esther Williams in an insignificant little musical, *Pagan Love Song*, then with Jane Wyman and Van Johnson in a comedy, *Three Guys Named Mike*. Neither film did much to help his career.

However, he next co-starred with Kathryn Grayson and Ava Gardner in one of his best pictures, *Showboat*. Keel remembers: "George Sidney, the director, wanted Katie and me to do a little waltz for the 'Why Do I Love You' number and wind up in the bedroom. Now, I knew how to waltz, but when Katie started to lead, we got all tangled up. A choreographer was called in, but we eventually cut the dancing and did the song sitting down."

After *Showboat,* Metro seemed to waste Keel's talent by casting him in such program pictures as *Texas Carnival, Lovely to Look At, Desperate Search* and *Fast Company.* "That's a perfect illustration of what my problem was at MGM," said Keel. "I'd do very well in movies like *Annie* and *Showboat,* but between these good vehicles, I'd be stuck in lemons, which would kill all the momentum I had going for me."

Prior to his doing *Kiss Me Kate* in 1953, Keel's spirits were at an all time low: "I was so depressed at that point. I'd done so many bad films that I felt I was on my way out."

The actor was not producer Jack Cummings' choice for the male lead in the Cole Porter musical. Cummings had wanted to bring Laurence Olivier over from England and dub in his singing voice. But Howard had good friends on the Metro lot in director George Sidney and Kathryn Grayson. At their insistence, Cummings allowed Keel to test for the 3-D film and, as a result, he won the role.

Keel readily admitted that: "Although it wasn't a big hit, *Kiss Me Kate* saved my career at that point."

Other musicals followed: *Rose Marie, Seven Brides for Seven Brothers* (his most successful picture), and *Kismet.* Then, in 1955, Metro dropped his contract. Big musicals weren't box-office anymore and the studio felt that finding other parts for Keel might be difficult. Undaunted, the performer started to free-lance.

One of Howard's more interesting post-Metro film roles was that of Simon-Peter in *The Big Fisherman* (1959). It was a demanding assignment and the actor's notices were good ones. "I did some of my best work in that picture," he says.

Another offbeat part was in a John Wayne/Kirk Douglas Western, *The War Wagon* (1967), in which he played an opportunistic Indian.

In the almost twenty years since he departed MGM, Howard Keel has seldom been idle. Films, television appearances, but especially nightclubs and stage work, keep him quite busy. One of the biggest draws on the summer stock circuit, Keel often entertains theatre audiences in such varied vehicles as *Man of La Mancha, Camelot, Kismet* and *Carousel.*

"Actually," he mused, "I prefer the stage; a live audience. As an actor, I find it a much more satisfying experience than films."

AND HE ALSO SAID:

"There was a caste system at Metro. I never got a big star dressing room until after *Seven Brides For Seven Brothers.*"

"I enjoyed working with Anthony Quinn and Ava Gardner on *Ride, Vaquero!*. In the gunfight scene, I kept outdrawing Tony when he was supposed to win."

"I was working at Douglas Aircraft, just singing on the side, when a psychic told me that I should be in show business full time. 'You'll have a slow start,' she said, 'then you'll go right to the top.'"

"When I broke my ankle on *Annie Get Your Gun,* they only had five shots of me in the can. I was afraid they might replace me, but producer Arthur Freed assured me that I would stay with the picture."

AFTERWORD:

Howard Keel made a major show business comeback in 1981 when he was cast as "Clayton Farlow" on the hit CBS television series, *Dallas.* He played the role until the series' demise in 1991.

He died in Palm Desert, California, of colon cancer on November 7, 2004. He was eighty-five years old.

Carl "Alfalfa" Switzer, Darla Hood, George "Spanky" McFarland

The Return of "The Little Rascals"

It seems that everybody I ran into back in the 1970s was an avid fan of the Our Gang/Little Rascals *comedies. At least, they talked as if they were.*

I first noted this kind of devotion in David, my four year old son, when he began eliminating words like "yes," "all right," and "okay" from his vocabulary in favor of "Oakie Doakie," the slang phrase that became the trademark of gang member "Spanky McFarland.

A passing phase, I thought, until David's mother started employing the expression. Evidently, she too had been watching the television reruns of these vintage two-reel comedies.

It wasn't long before I began hearing "Oakie Doakie" from my barber, insurance agent, business associates, sales clerks and even a telephone operator. Perhaps the whole world was regressing back to childhood.

Ergo, I was well primed when my editor suggested that I devote an installment of "Yesterday at the Movies" to the Our Gang *kids and what had become of them. You see, she had experienced the power of the* Little Rascals *phenomenon also. Her children, and especially her husband, had all joined the cult.*

On a personal note: When I was in high school back in Seattle, I spent Saturdays, summers and the holiday season working in a pawn shop owned by the father of Billy Wolfstone, who played secondary roles in the Our Gang *films during the early 1930s. Bill was then a Seattle businessman and he stopped by the store every now and then.*

Because I interviewed several people, this was the longest column I wrote for Coronet. *I met in person with Darla Hood and Matthew "Stymie" Beard and did phone interviews with "Fat" Joe Cobb and director Gordon Douglas. The story appeared in the September 1974 issue of* Coronet *and was later reprinted in* Liberty Magazine.

Created by producer Hal Roach, the *Our Gang* comedies had a 22-year production run from 1922 through mid-1944. 176 kids played in the series during its lifetime, including Jackie Cooper, Dickie Moore, Nanette Fabray, Eddie Bracken, Johnny Downs, Darryl Hickman and Robert Blake (known then as "Mickey Gubitosi") – all of whom went on to individual stardom. Ironically, Shirley Temple had tried out for the films, but was turned down.

The more popular youngsters stayed an average of five years with the series or until they got too big for their parts. Roach tried to maintain the same basic types in each succeeding "generation" of kids (i.e. a black child, a pudgy one, and so forth).

"Fat" Joe Cobb, the first chubby youngster in the series, began with Roach in 1922 at age five. Recently, he told us how his career began: "My dad and I were visiting in Los Angeles from Oklahoma when we learned that Mr. Roach was looking for kids. We borrowed a car to drive out to the studio and arrived at the start of the lunch break. The casting people took us out to eat with them, then after lunch, they took me back to the studio and that same day they put me into a comedy with Charlie Chase and Snub Pollard. Right after that, I became a member of the *Our Gang* kids."

Cobb earned $750 per week as a member of the company and stayed with the series through its first few talkies. Unfortunately, all of the sound films in which he appeared were destroyed by fire.

For the past twenty-eight years, Cobb has worked in the maintenance department of Rockwell International in Los Angeles. He still has that roly-poly look, standing 4'10" and weighing in at 145 pounds.

Matthew "Stymie" Beard was the third black youngster to appear in the series, succeeding "Sunshine Sammy" Morrison (now a worker in the missile/aerospace industry) and Allen "Farina" Hoskins (the director of a psychiatric workshop in Northern California).

Beard recalled how he garnered his nickname: "I was a curious kid and was so excited about being on a movie lot that I kept getting into things, looking under piles of boards at the wrong time; standing in people's way. One day, the director got so frustrated that he said I 'stymied' him, and the name stuck."

Beard considered his five years with the series to be one of the happiest periods of his life: "We had fun doing the films. The kids got along very well and, aside from an occasional scrap, there were no problems.

"Working right next to us on the lot were people like Charlie Chase, Patsy Kelly and, of course, Laurel and Hardy. Stan and Ollie used to come over to our set. They'd play with us kids and buy us ice cream cones. It was a great time for me."

Yet, for "Stymie," the series had its drawbacks: "One picture we did had a mayonnaise fight in it and we were covered with the stuff for days. In another short, we had to eat dozens of artichokes. I still can't stand those foods."

Beard's life after *Our Gang* was plagued with troubles. In his late teens, he tried marijuana, then while serving a jail term, "Stymie" was introduced to "hard" drugs. The years 1957-63 were spent in prison for possession and sale of heroin. However, through the help of the Synanon Foundation, Beard seemed to have straightened out his life and has successfully begun to re-establish himself in the acting profession.

Scotty Beckett, another gang member who got involved with drugs, died of an overdose in 1968.

Gordon Douglas had been associated with the *Our Gang* comedies for a number of years in various capacities – casting director, assistant director, gag writer – when, in 1936, Roach allowed the young man to make his directorial debut on the series' first one-reel short, *Bored of Education.* To everyone's surprise, the picture won the Oscar that year as Best Short Subject.

Douglas remembered: "I figured that if at twenty-two I could win an Academy Award, I had this town made."

After directing several more segments of the series over the next two years, Douglas went on to feature films, accumulating such credits as *Come Fill the Cup, Them!, Tony Rome* and *The Detective.*

"It was like a family on the *Our Gang* series," reflected Douglas. "They were all wonderful kids, all different, and you had to handle each one in a particular way. Some you'd push, some you'd kiss or pet, others you'd just give a kick in the ass.

"They were good youngsters, fun to be around. In fact, I used to take them out on Saturdays when we weren't working."

To avoid perennial stage mothers, Douglas had a firm rule on the set. A rope was used to divide the area where shooting was taking place and the rest of the sound stage. A sign on the rope read: "Parents Not Permitted Beyond This Point."

The best known "generation" of kids –and those seen most often on television – included George "Spanky" McFarland, Carl "Alfalfa" Switzer, Billy "Buckwheat" Thomas, Eugene "Porky" Lee, Darla Hood and Pete, the dog with the circle around his eye.

Darla Hood, now the wife of music publisher José Granson, lives in the San Fernando Valley. Her voice can regularly be heard on various television commercials, including the often-played "Chicken-of-the-Sea" spot of a few years back.

Darla started with the *Our Gang* comedies in 1936 at age 3 1/2 and stayed with it until her 12th birthday. "They gave me a big party at the studio," she recalled, "then told me I was 'out'."

Her years with the series, nevertheless, were enjoyable: " I didn't realize

I was working in pictures. I loved to do what the directors told me to do – wearing costumes and having fun – but I didn't know I was a movie star. I was eleven years old before I saw myself in films."

The author interviews a grown-up Darla Hood

Miss Hood admits that "Alfalfa" was quite the prankster on the set.: "I used to get so angry at him. He'd do things like put soap flakes in the cream puffs we were eating or slip fish hooks into Spanky's pockets.

"Live fish always used to scare me and there was one film we did where all the kids were to fall into what we thought was an empty fish pond. Well, 'Alfalfa' put fish in it and when I felt them swimming over me, I just stood up and screamed."

Following her departure, Darla had a comparatively easy time adapting to the world away from the studio: "My only major difficulty came in school, because I had trouble associating with people not in show business. Except for Baby Patsy, I'd been the only girl in the series and, at first, I really didn't know how to play with other girls my own age."

Darla Hood had only one regret about the series: "None of us get any residuals from the films being played on television."

Tracing the subsequent lives of the various *Our Gang* kids is not an easy task, since most of them did not stay in contact with each other after the series folded in 1944. Also, according to Miss Hood: "There were a lot of imposters around who claim to have been one or another of the kids."

Many conflicting reports exist as to the fate of Billy Thomas. One informant says that "Buckwheat" has been working for a Los Angeles record company for the past fifteen years. From other sources, we learned that the former actor became a career army man, who was killed in 1968 while flying food into Biafra. (*According to the IMDb, Thomas died in Los Angeles of a heart attack on October 10, 1980*).

Eugene "Porky" Lee joined the teaching profession, but his whereabouts are unknown. (*The IMDb reports that Lee died in Minneapolis, Minnesota, on October 16, 2005 of lung and brain cancer.*)

George "Spanky" McFarland, described by director Douglas as being "a kid with a good brain that the other youngsters looked up to," bounced from job-to-job for several years, but is now a distributor for Philco/Ford in Texas. (*The IMDb states that McFarland died of a heart attack on June 30, 1993.*)

Perhaps the most tragic member of the troupe was Carl "Alfalfa" Switzer. While working in Los Angeles as a bartender, he was shot to death in 1959 during an argument over a $50 debt.

José Granson, Darla Hood's husband, made the observation: "A lot of these kids went wrong as adults because they were just plain frustrated. They'd received nothing but adoration as children. Unfortunately, they couldn't go back to that. There wasn't the protection of the studio anymore and coping with the world outside was too difficult. So, they tried drugs, fly-by-night schemes, and the like."

No matter what eventual fate befell these youngsters, it still does not detract from our enjoyment of watching them during their happier, more innocent years. Television has provided for this. Throughout the country, stations run the timeless *Our Gang* (retitled *The Little Rascals*) comedies nightly.

For our children, the films help them to utilize their imaginations; to identify with other kids their own age. But, for us, the comedies provide a nostalgic look backward at our own childhood. Or, at least, how we wish it might have been.

AND THEY ALSO SAID:

"Fat" Joe Cobb:

"I always thought I'd like to get into commercials, but I didn't try. I never worked enough."

❧

Matthew "Stymie" Beard:

" 'Oakie Doakie': Spanky started that word."

❧

"I got involved through my Dad. He had a couple of parking lots downtown. A lawyer told him that Roach was looking for a new black kid because 'Farina' hat gotten too tall. I didn't even have to test. I just walked onto the lot and the casting guy said: 'That's the kid. Sign him for five years.'

"I stayed until I outgrew the part."

❧

"The studio wanted me to have a bald head. I always had a bald head. I'm not used to hair. It itches."

❧

"After I left the series, I did *Captain Blood* with Errol Flynn. I played the houseboy."

❧

Gordon Douglas:

"They were great kids. Unfortunately, many of them turned out to be bad."

❧

"Buckwheat" started strutting around after Joe Louis won the heavyweight title. He thought he was tough.

"Then, we did a film where he had to crawl along the deck of a metal boat. We didn't realize it was a hot deck until he started crying. It burned his hands."

❧

"Spanky was older than the rest. He was smart. The other kids looked up to him."

❧

Darla Hood:

"Kids today can't believe that we're grown up. They still write fan letters."

❧

"'Alfalfa' was spoiled; a beast. His parents treated him like a god. He would deliberately ruin takes. He would pinch me, so that I would cry when I was supposed to be happy.

❧

"In one movie, he dropped me into Toluca Lake when he was supposed to be saving me. I've been scared of water ever since."

"Buckwheat" was a lovely person. His father passed away while we were working on the films. He was crushed."

"The mothers taught the boys to be nice to me because I was the only girl. I was lonely.

"We did one film where midgets join the gang. I thought the midget lady was a little girl. She acted like a little girl, and I was thrilled to have another little girl on the set with me. It was years later before I learned she was really a little person."

"The greatest thing that happened: I met 'Uncle' Clark Gable."

AFTERWORD:

"Fat" Joe Cobb died from natural causes in Santa Ana, California, on May 21, 2002.

Matthew "Stymie" Beard passed away from pneumonia in Los Angeles on January 8, 1981.

Gordon Douglas died of cancer in Los Angeles on September 29, 1993.

Darla Hood died in Hollywood on June 13, 1979. Cause of death was acute hepatitis.

Gale Sondergaard

Gale Sondergaard

I honestly don't recall how my editor and I decided that I should interview Gale Sondergaard for my column. Perhaps I'd just seen her recently on television in a movie. I don't really remember.

In any event, we met at the Hollywood Brown Derby and we seemed to have an immediate rapport. For me, it was a very enjoyable two hours of conversation.

The interview appeared in the October 1974 issue of Coronet.

"People seem to remember me for the evil roles I played," reflected Gale Sondergaard in our interview at a Hollywood restaurant.

"Fans forget fine films like *The Letter* and *The Life of Emile Zola* when they request an autograph and only mention *The Spider Woman Strikes Back*, a movie that I didn't want to do and would, frankly, like to forget. But, they won't let me because the picture has now become 'camp'.

"I guess that villains remain more dominant in the minds of an audience. They're usually more colorful than the hero and, from an acting standpoint, more fun to play."

Born in Litchfield, Minnesota, in 1900, Miss Sondergaard had no thought of going into the theatre until her high school English teacher suggested it. The future actress had moved the woman to tears with a dramatic speech she'd performed before her class.

Following her college education and a period of time doing stock in Detroit, Gale headed for New York where she saw Lynn Fontanne starring in Eugene O'Neill's *Strange Interlude*: "It was the most exciting play I'd ever seen and I said to myself, 'That's my role'. I studied the part and, eventually, was set as standby for Miss Fontanne's replacement, Judith Anderson. Later, I inherited the role. Got to play it for six months."

Hollywood beckoned her at this point in her career, but Gale ignored the offers: "I was a snob. I felt that working in movies was not really acting. I didn't even go out to be interviewed by the studio representatives."

Instead, she signed a three-year contract with the Theatre Guild. Her husband, director Herbert Biberman, was also with that group and it was because of his desire to move to the West Coast, in order to establish a name for himself in films, that Gale decided to make the "noble sacrifice" and go with him: "I was ready to give up my acting career to be with Herbert, but I still didn't want to do movie roles, as I didn't think I belonged in pictures. I wasn't glamorous enough for Hollywood."

The studios continued to pursue her. So, after a few months of taking life easy, she went to see director Mervyn LeRoy regarding the role of Faith in *Anthony Adverse*. Bette Davis had originally been slated for that assignment, but Warner Brothers ultimately decided that the secondary part should go to an unknown and Miss Sondergaard got the nod.

The adventure classic, starring Fredric March, Olivia deHavilland and Claude Rains, was a tremendous success and Gale was voted the Oscar as Best Supporting Actress of 1936 – the first performer to win in this newly established awards category.

Other good roles followed: Lucie Dreyfus in *The Life of Emile Zola* with Paul Muni; the Empress Eugenie in *Juarez* starring Muni and Bette Davis ("I liked that part because history tells us she was the force behind Napoleon III, who pushed him into sending Maximilian into Mexico."); Inez in *The Mark of Zorro* with Tyrone Power; and, of course, the mysterious Eurasian woman from *The Letter* starring Bette Davis again.

"William Wyler, the director, and I had a bit of a dispute on how I should play the part in *The Letter*," recalled Miss Sondergaard. "I went in to be fitted for costumes and found that Wyler had already picked out several rather blatant and tasteless outfits for me to wear.

"I asked Willie, 'Why should this person be played as a person of the gutter? Because she's half Chinese? She actually has a higher standard of morals than Bette Davis' character, who is an adulteress, as well as a murderess.'

"Willie thought about my argument overnight, then the next morning, he admitted that I'd been right. He went along with my way of thinking and the part was played with dignity."

It's a little known fact that Gale Sondergaard was the original actress cast to play the wicked witch in *The Wizard of Oz*: "The original idea was for me to play a glamorous witch, however shortly before filming began, producer Mervyn LeRoy came to me and said that the studio heads had changed their minds and wanted the role to have an 'ugly' makeup. They felt, and probably rightfully so, that this new interpretation would be more frightening to children. I, of course, refused to do the part that way and Margaret Hamilton replaced me."

The 1940s found Gale doing roles in such projects as *The Blue Bird* with Shirley Temple; *The Spider Woman*, a Sherlock Holmes mystery with Basil Rathbone, which inspired *The Spider Woman Strikes Back*; *Road to Rio* starring Bing Crosby and Bob Hope; and *Anna and the King of Siam*, the Irene Dunne-Rex Harrison film, for which Miss Sondergaard's role of Lady Thiang garnered her a second Oscar nomination.

When, in 1947, the House UnAmerican Activities Committee named her husband, Herbert Biberman, as one of the ill-fated "Hollywood Ten," Gale Sondergaard was also "blacklisted" in the entertainment industry. Months before, her talents had been very much in demand. But, after the hearings, neither the actress, nor her husband, were able to find work.

"It was a terrible time," she remembered. "We were luckier than most of the 'blacklisted' artists. We, at least, were financially secure."

To keep busy during the ensuing years, Gale put together a one-woman show, which she called *Woman and Her Emergence into Fuller Status as a Human Being in Relation to Her Male.* The presentation consisted of a series of dramatic speeches (such as from Ibsen's *A Doll's House*) dealing with the rights of women. It was performed by the actress at colleges and universities around the country and might rightly be considered a forerunner to the "woman's lib" movement.

"I've always been out-spoken for women's rights, " she admitted. "I got that from my mother. She used to march in suffrage parades."

Today, the "blacklist" is virtually forgotten and its victims, for the most part, have been exonerated. Miss Sondergaard, who was widowed a couple of years ago, has returned to her profession, spending the majority of her time working in the theatre. Television audiences saw her last season when she co-starred in an ABC-TV movie, *The Cat Creature,* playing of all things, another villainess.

Unlike many who were "blacklisted," Gale speaks freely about her years in "exile": "I'm proud that I was part of that period. People had to take a stand back then and I'm glad that my husband and I had the courage to do so.

"The real losers were the public. They were denied the talents of some truly great artists for nearly twenty years."

Gale Sondergaard – At 74, she still doesn't hesitate to speak what's on her mind. She's really quite a remarkable lady.

AND SHE ALSO SAID:

"My father was a dairy, butter expert; later a professor of agriculture at the University of Wisconsin. But, we never lived on a farm."

"Mother taught me piano until I rebelled at age twelve.

"She was a frustrated career woman,
but she bred independence into me."

❧

"When I work, I work very professionally. I don't make close friends in movies, as in the theatre. There's just not the same feeling of 'family'."

❧

"I enjoy doing comedy. I did four movies with Bob Hope. I would come home from the set with my ribs aching from laughing."

❧

"There are many men's roles that can be done by a woman. My role in *The Cat Creature* was originally written for a man."

❧

"People think I was in *Rebecca* because I always played housekeepers. I wasn't. That was Judith Anderson."

❧

"Luise Rainer 's role in *The Good Earth* is a part that I wanted."

❧

"Being 'blacklisted' gave me the opportunity to be a mother to my children."

❧

"Right now, I'm just following the bends in the river."

AFTERWORD:

Gale Sondergaard died in Woodland Hills, California, on August 14, 1985 from cerebral vascular thrombosis. She was eighty-six years old.

Other Interviews

Yvonne DeCarlo

Yvonne De Carlo

My interview with Yvonne DeCarlo was an assignment from National Enquirer. *As I recall, they wanted her to talk about her diet, but I found the other things she had to say far more interesting.*

Although I really didn't write about it in my article and didn't take many notes on the subject, the one thing that sticks in my mind about the time we spent together is that what Ms. DeCarlo wanted to talk about most were all the lovers she'd had in her life, including Howard Hughes.

It was a fascinating couple of hours, but National Enquirer *didn't like the piece I wrote because it didn't concentrate on the actress' diet. They paid me a "kill fee," and that was that.*

Here's the piece that they turned down.

"I'm a terrific mother," claimed Yvonne DeCarlo in a recent candid interview at the Beverly Hills Brown Derby.

"I'm a mother first and an actress second. I'd do anything for my children, including die for them. But, I'm not so sure I'd do that for my husband or any of the lovers I've had in the past."

Dressed in a red pants suit and wearing a polo hat over hair stll wet from a swim, Hollywood's sexy siren of the 1940s and 50s was reflecting on her life, both personal and professional, since her popular television series, *The Munsters,* was cancelled in 1966.

"I did *Follies* in New York a couple of years ago. Broadway's very nice if you're impressed with that kind of life, which I'm not. It doesn't pay well unless you're Ethel Merman. Nevertheless, it's great exposure and it gives you the opportunity to prove you can sing and dance."

Indeed, Miss DeCarlo enjoys singing much more than she does straight acting and, since leaving *Follies,* she has performed *No, No, Nanette* for nine months in both Australia and New Zealand; a Cole Porter revue in San Diego; and will soon embark on a dinner theatre tour doing *Dames at Sea.*

"These dinner theaters are a good idea," she says. "It gives people who ordinarily don't go to plays the opportunity to do so. For a relatively small amount of money, they get a nice dinner and see a star like Mickey Rooney, Forrest Tucker, or myself in a condensed version of a Broadway hit."

Despite her busy schedule, Miss DeCarlo gets her greatest pleasure out of being with her two sons by former stuntman Robert Morgan, to whom she has been married since 1955. (Morgan had his stunting career cut short when, during the filming of the 1962 film *How the West Was Won,* he was involved in an accident that resulted in his leg being amputated.) The family lives in Beverly Hills on Coldwater Drive.

At 17, son Bruce is active in swimming competition, having just made all-city high school finals. Michael (16), on the other hand, enjoys motorcycle racing. Says their mother: "I'm proud of my boys. They're so dedicated. Bruce even shaves his arms, so he can get more speed in the water."

On the Sunday following this interview, Michael was planning to enter a cycle race out in the desert and, like any parent would be, Yvonne was a bit nervous about it: "Naturally, I get worried when he races. But, I have to let him do his 'thing.' It's funny, there's so much speed competition in my life now."

"I never wanted to have girls," she muses, "only boys. I'm really not sure that I like the female sex, including female dogs.

"Sure, I have close girl friends, like Ava Gardner and Princess Grace, but they're *real* dames, not phony. Most women aren't like that."

She was born Peggy Yvonne Middleton in Vancouver, British Columbia, in 1922. When she entered pictures, playing a bit in the Alan Ladd classic, *This Gun for Hire,* Yvonne adopted the DeCarlo moniker, which was her mother's maiden name.

Yvonne's break came when producer Walter Wanger cast her in the title role of his 1945 film, *Salome, Where She Danced*: "Wanger saw me sitting in his reception room and was startled by the fact that I looked like his wife, actress Joan Bennett. So, that got me in to see him and the part was mine."

A series of exotic roles in "B" pictures followed – *Slave Girl, River Lady, The Desert Hawk* and *Sea Devils* – until, in the mid-1950s, the actress got two plumb assignments – Charlton Heston's wife in Cecil B. DeMille's *The Ten Commandments* and the lead opposite Clark Gable and relative newcomer Sidney Poitier in *Band of Angels.* Unfortunately, neither of these parts gave her the career boost that she'd hoped for and Yvonne continued to appear in program pictures until she was signed for *The Munsters* series in 1964. That successful show, co-starring Fred Gwynne, ran for two years and inspired a theatrical feature, *Munster, Go Home!*

"I've been offered many good parts," she confessed, "but the trouble is that I'm never around. I'm always on the road and somebody else gets cast."

Her most recent movie work consists of a cameo role in the still unreleased feature, *Arizona Slim,* filmed a few months ago in New York. [NOTE: In checking the *IMDb,* although it is listed, it does not appear that this film was ever released.]

Today, Miss DeCarlo's favorite pastime is driving a car on the open highway: "Wherever I travel, I always rent a car. I drove all over Australia when I was there. For me, driving is a release; a feeling of freedom, an escape."

The performer feels that she still must continue working and was, therefore, pleased when her doctor, following a routine check-up last week, gave her a clean bill of health.

"I know it's silly," she said, " but in a way, it was rather disappointing. You spend a couple of hundred dollars for the examination and you'd think they could find *something.*"

Yvonne freely admits that she, occasionally, has problems with her weight: "I get bored with dieting. There are so many gimmicks these days – shots from the urine of a pregnant woman, massage, wrapping in bandages – I think they're all ridiculous. I tried a low-carbohydrate diet once. It worked for awhile, but then it stopped.

"I don't know. Maybe I'll stop eating altogether. But, then I'd get cranky and be miserable to be around, so I guess, the best way to go about it would be to get away by myself when I want to diet, probably to the mountains.

"You really need a reason to lose weight, whether it be to get in shape for a professional engagement or to make yourself attractive for a lover. Otherwise, even the best diet won't work."

Another of the actress' interests is writing. She created a major portion of the material for her nightclub act, which she's performed both here and abroad, and also wrote an outline for a motion picture: "I showed it to Alec Guinness when we were filming *The Captain's Paradise*, but I told him it was by some Hollywood writer. He said he liked it. Then, I revealed the truth and he seemed disappointed."

Some day, Yvonne would like to find the time to write a book of children's fairy tales, but is unsure if she has the imagination to make the project work.

As far as the future is concerned, Miss DeCarlo hopes to star in her *own* Broadway musical ("If Alexis Smith can get her own show, so can I.") and, of greater interest, would like to do a "talk" show: "It would be fun to be like Barbara Walters; have a television program in which I did news, interviews and commentary."

Has she ever considered writing her autobiography?

"Several times. But, I believe in the truth and I believe that all my lovers would have to be dead before I could reveal the story of my life."

AND SHE ALSO SAID:

"I don't have faith in people because people are the way they are."

"Everything I do is fun and interesting."

"It's difficult for a woman to work clubs in Australia. There are too many costume changes, and you go to two clubs every night. You spend half your time driving across town."

"After we danced together in *Criss Cross,* Tony Curtis and I became buddies. He was so intense to *make it* in the business. 'I'm going to *make it*' he'd always say.

"We dated like buddies; pals. I wonder if he remembers how close we were."

"My husband, Bob, was a stuntman on *How the West Was Won* when he had his accident. He fell beneath a train and the cars ran over him several times.

"He died on the operating table three times. It took over a year to bring him back. He's a strong-willed man. He went through therapy, which was difficult; got depressed that he was incapacitated.

"Now, he wears an artificial leg, does an occasional movie and is active in golf tournaments. He's coped well with it."

AFTERWORD:

During our conversation, Miss DeCarlo told me *off the record* that she might be divorcing her husband in the not-too-distant-future. I assured her that this information would not appear in the story I was writing. "I don't know what's going to happen," she said. "We've been apart for years because I travel. The thing's really over, but I don't know if we're going to separate. I'd rather not talk about it."

The couple divorced in 1973.

Their son, Michael, died in 1997 from unknown causes, though the police did say it was possible "foul play."

Morgan died in 1999.

Yvonne DeCarlo passed away of "natural causes" at the Motion Picture Home in Woodland Hills on January 8, 2007. She was 84 and had previously suffered a stroke.

David Janssen

David Janssen

My interview with David Janssen was a Coronet *assignment that was never published, probably because it came at a time when the magazine was shifting around its editorial staff and there was a miscommunication on what emphasis in the story the new editor wanted.*

I lunched with Janssen and a studio publicist at a restaurant in Universal City, and I certainly enjoyed chatting with the actor who had a remarkable dry sense of humor.

The interview took place while Janssen was filming the second half of the first season of his series, Harry O, *which had recently shifted its location from San Diego to Los Angeles.*

My friend and former publicity client, Henry Darrow, co-starred on Harry O *before I'd met him. He'd played Janssen's police detective buddy. So, the other day, I phoned Henry, who now lives in North Carolina, and asked him why the show had switched locations.*

"It was too expensive to shoot in San Diego," he said. "We even had to import union extras from Los Angeles. Also, the City Council was not that cooperative. They made it very difficult for us to shoot on the locations we needed."

Since Darrow was playing a San Diego cop, script-wise it made no sense for him to stay with the show when Janssen's character moved to Los Angeles mid-season. "However, they did pay me for the entire season," Darrow said.

Here is the interview that did not *run in* Coronet.

"I spent six years playing the leading man's best friend or the best friend's best friend," recalled David Janssen about his early career under contract to Universal Pictures.

The handsome star of *Harry O*, ABC-TV's popular private-eye series, had been signed for the Universal New Talent Program in 1950, after doing an "interview" screen test: "I'd done a scene for Sophie Rosenstein, who was then head of New Talent, and she was impressed enough to order this ridiculous test in which you faced the camera and answered questions while, at the same time, trying to exhibit some sort of screen personality."

The top male stars at the studio during the fifties were Rock Hudson, Tony Curtis, Jeff Chandler and Audie Murphy, but several of the young men in the new talent program were later to make their marks in either movies or television. Janssen, Dennis Weaver, Richard Long, Jack Kelly and Clint Eastwood all went on to greater stardom *after* they left the Universal fold.

"As far as I was concerned," admitted Janssen, "I don't think I ever fit the mold for their pictures, so they used me as an 'agreer'. In other words, the leading man had a problem in the film and would, ultimately, come up with a plan on how to solve it. I, being one of his silent buddies, would, naturally, give my approval, then disappear from the picture

"From a creative standpoint, it was very frustrating to be a contract actor back then because you knew that the only thing the studio expected of you was to show up."

Indeed, Janssen felt that the 50s was a very imitative period for movies. Pictures copied the look of the forties and had a fantasized approach to life: "Really, not much was required of actors then and, therefore, the studios went more for 'types' than 'talent'. You'll note that very few actors who became stars through the studio talent programs of that era have survived in the business.

"In Universal's case, they were forced to draw upon their contract people because all of the *big* names were over at Metro or Fox and the powers at the studio didn't want to pay the tremendous fees demanded for borrowing one of them.

"In fact, Universal was so structured that most of its scripts were written around standing sets. One stage housed the old galleon, which they used over and over again for pirate movies.

"We had a joke back then about a writer whose script opened on a moat, then dissolved to a dungeon, then cut to the New York Street. When he was asked how he could justify a moat, a dungeon and the New York Street in the same movie, he'd say, 'I'll work it into a dream sequence.'"

Janssen's mother was a former Ziegfeld girl, who traveled the country with that showman's *Rio Rita*. Once she settled in Hollywood, it was her idea that her son become a child star. Muses the actor: "I really wasn't that interested in films until I got into college. However, I went along with my mother because I found acting was a much easier way to make money than working in a grocery store or mowing lawns."

In 1957, a year after he'd been dropped by the studio, Janssen was signed by actor/producer Dick Powell to star as television's *Richard Diamond, Detective*, a role the former crooner had originated on radio. Janssen reflected: "I was very flattered that Powell had chosen me to play his part. It was the first time the total responsibility for a project fell on my shoulders.

"It's funny but, although the production techniques for *Richard Diamond* were rather primitive by today's standards, the concept for that kind of private-eye show is still with us. It's the approach where the hero kills fifteen heavies with one shot, and he always has a great humorous reply for any question.

"With *Harry O*, we're trying to go more in the opposite direction; to play the episodes with more reality and believable solutions."

The series that made the name of David Janssen a household word was ABC's *The Fugitive*, in which he portrayed "Dr. Richard Kimble," a wrongly accused wife murderer on the lam. A major hit for four seasons beginning in 1963, the program's final segment, in which the real killer was apprehended, earned the year's highest viewer rating – after the Academy Awards and the initial running of *The Bridge on the River Kwai*.

"When it was decided that we weren't going to do the series for a fifth season," Janssen said, "we had a long meeting to plan what the wrap-up would be. Some people felt that we should have a surprise ending; possibly with even 'Inspector Gerard' being the murderer. But, ultimately, we felt that we couldn't disappoint our viewers who'd been loyal for so many years, so we stayed with the one-armed man as the villain."

Janssen has also appeared often on the motion picture screen – *The Shoes of the Fisherman, Generation* (garnering excellent reviews in one of the few projects in which he's been allowed to play comedy), *Marooned*, and *King of the Roaring Twenties* (as mobster Arnold Rothstein) being among his better assignments in this medium. Forthcoming is the pivotal role of "Tom Cole" in Paramount's production of Jacqueline Susann's *Once Is Not Enough.*

Often compared in looks to Clark Gable, the performer had no desire to play the "King" in Universal's announced biography, *Gable and Lombard*: "First of all, I'm too old for the years of Gable's life that they're planning to portray but, most important, I think that anybody who attempts that part is going to be faced with a stiff, unflattering comparison." (James Brolin wound up playing Gable in the poorly received 1976 film and Jill Clayburgh was Carole Lombard.)

Whereas some of the early episodes of *Harry O* were on the weak side, Janssen was very happy with his new series and how its stories have improved over the weeks to make the show one of the most successful of the new season: "With television, you need a season to find your way in a series. Good ideas in an office discussion or in a script don't always come off when they're filmed. It's unfortunate that the networks don't always go along with some of the slow starting programs because, I think, that many of them have had good potential."

As far as "dreams for the future" are concerned, Janssen would like to branch out and play a variety of roles: "I sometimes get depressed when I think I'm just 'spinning my wheels'. Successful actors can get thrown into a mold; a way of life that doesn't seem productive. Money is a great seducer and can be responsible for getting you 'typed'. You wake up one morning and say 'nobody thinks I can do anything else.'"

The actor continues: "One always wants to make a contribution for 'eternity'. In my case, I'd like to be in a definitive motion picture; something that will go down in history as one of the 'great' films."

Looking at the other side of the coin, Janssen notes: "It's gratifying to know that you've come this far in the business, through bad and good films, and still managed to survive. Perhaps its just been a matter of sheer 'guts'. Anyway, it helps to think of that when you start putting yourself down too much."

David Janssen is a man who enjoys people and it's evident that he's not let success go to his head: "How can you do that when you've gone step-by-step over the years to get there. It doesn't change you as it might if you'd made it overnight. After all, I wasn't 'discovered' at a soda fountain."

AND HE ALSO SAID:

> "Parents can only live vicariously through their children when the offspring are young. That's the only time it's really rewarding to them, because after they're grown, the kids are responsible for their own success and failures and the older generation can no longer take credit for them. Of course, they can beam with pride that that's their boy or girl, but it's not the same."

> "When I was doing *The Fugitive*, the networks were much more puritanical than today. Already on *Harry O*, I've had two affairs, one of which was not implied. On the other hand, how can the network let the expression 'son-of-a-bitch' stay when they air *Patton*, yet refuse to let us use it on our show? Hell, those daytime soap operas deal with much stronger subject matter than we've been allowed. There's just too much of a double-standard on television today."

AFTERWORD:

David Janssen died of a heart attack in Malibu, California, on February 13, 1980. He was forty-eight years old.

Gary Cooper in *High Noon*

High Noon

This piece was, apparently, a pilot article for a new column I was trying to peddle, "Behind the Scenes with The Great Movies." Truthfully, I don't remember to whom I was tying to peddle it or even if I did, indeed, sell it.

I don't even remember meeting Elmo Williams, but I do have my interview notes, so I assume it was a phone interview.

In any case, I think it's an interesting, informative little article. Enjoy!

Two-time Academy Award winner Gary Cooper would not have won his 1952 Oscar for *High Noon* had it not been for the skill of a film editor.

"Coop was in constant pain from a recent hernia operation," recalled Elmo Williams, who cut the classic Western movie. "As a result, he had trouble concentrating on his performance."

High Noon tells the story of a newly married marshal who, deserted by his townspeople, must face alone four gunmen out to kill him. As the clock hands draw closer to the appointed time of the showdown, the strain on the peace officer becomes apparent; "Cooper's portrayal was inconsistent. It just didn't show the growing concern for his character's plight," said the editor.

Williams, later a producer (*Tora! Tora! Tora!*), did "major surgery" on the actor's performance, as well as on the film itself: "I cut the picture down to its bare bones, and then some.

"Initially, the story had several subplots, all dealing with possible outside help coming to aid Cooper. One tale showed a boy riding to fetch his father to come to town and join the posse. But, the horse fell and the kid broke his leg, so that assistance never came.

"Another subplot concerned one of the marshal's deputies, played by

James Brown, bringing a prisoner into town. Unfortunately, the outlaw escaped, shooting the deputy in the process. So, that assistance never arrived either. There were a couple of other similar side stories also."

In editing the footage for the Stanley Kramer/Carl Foreman production, Williams noted that every time the action cut away from what was happening in town, "the story went to pieces." Additionally, he thought that director Fred Zinnemann had spent too much time building the character of the marshal's wife, who was being played by Grace Kelly. "I felt that her part was a relatively minor aspect of the story and should be put into perspective."

After he'd viewed the first cut, a discouraged Kramer was on the verge of shelving the picture when Williams talked the producer into letting him work on the project over the weekend to see what he could do.

"Once I'd eliminated the side stories," reflected the cutter, "the tension in the film, naturally, increased. I built the suspense even further by continually cutting away to the railroad station where the killers were waiting. I also increased the sound of the clock. After that, I got to work on Cooper's performance, rearranging his scenes, thus his nervousness appeared to grow more logically."

Williams ran into another problem. He discovered that Zinnemann had arranged his camera angles in order to have a clock in almost every shot: "When I started changing scenes around, I found ways to trick the audience, so they wouldn't notice that time was moving both backward and forward from sequence to sequence."

Wanting to make the film almost a folktale, Williams obtained a recording of Burl Ives' "Ghost Riders in the Sky," then got an actor friend to read a narration over it. This was played for Kramer when the latter saw the revised cut on Monday morning.

The producer liked Williams' ideas and ordered him to complete the picture along the lines he had begun. Ned Washington and Dimitri Tiomkin were commissioned to write a ballad, which was to be sung throughout the film by Tex Ritter, and as they say, the rest is history.

"Actually," said Williams, "they never released the best version of *High*

Noon. That one ran 76 minutes. But, United Artists needed a longer picture if it was to go out as the top half of the bill. Accordingly, I stuck back in nine minutes, which had to do with the Cooper/Katy Jurado relationship."

The Western masterpiece won Academy Awards for Best Actor, Best Song and, of course, Best Editing.

Williams' Oscar was well deserved. Without him, there wouldn't have been a *High Noon.*

AND HE ALSO SAID:

"Another of the side stories that we cut involved a friend of Cooper's on his way back into town, who stops to jump into the sack with a girl, played by Roberta Hayes."

"At first, Stanley Kramer wasn't enthralled with my cut, but he loved it later. Zinnemann was happy with the final film, but angry with me when we were doing it."

"I had a certain amount of freedom back then, which is no longer possible in the industry."

"Work for what goes with the film and everything else will fall into place."

AFTERWORD:

Elmo Williams died of heart problems on November 25, 2015 in Brookings, Oregon. He was 102 years old.

The Books

Producer Stanley Rubin, the author, and
Mrs. Rubin (actress Kathleen Hughes)

Make It Again, Sam

Published in 1975, Make It Again, Sam *was, I believe, the first book that dealt exclusively with the practice of movie remakes.*

The good news is that the book sold well and major film critics of the day (e.g. Arthur Knight, Pauline Kael) kept a copy on their desks to use as reference.

The bad news is that, even before the book hit the bookstores, it was out-of-date. Indeed, virtually every book that deals with a continuing phenomenon, like movie remakes, faces that problem.

The joy in writing this book, as well as other works about Hollywood and the movies, is that it gave me the opportunity to meet and chat with many of the legendary actors, producers, directors and writers who lived and worked in the film industry during its Golden Era. Sadly, these people are no longer with us, but what follows are some of the things that they said to me about the movies they made and their remakes.

Stanley Rubin

(Producer of *Destry,* a remake of *Destry Rides Again*)

"If a studio is going to remake an old film – especially a successful one – they better have something in mind that will make the new picture better than the original.

"For example, maybe the theme is timely again, or perhaps, there's a 'hot' piece of casting that makes the project an exciting one.

"Universal wanted to redo *Destry Rides Again*[1] as a vehicle for Audie Murphy, who was under contract and was a good box-office property. I wasn't too excited about the project – mainly because Murphy was not a first-rate actor and I didn't want to do a remake. The fact that George Marshall was agreeable to come back and direct this new version was a major reason why I decided to go ahead with it.

"Marshall is the best comedy/action director in the business. He was marvelous at updating and switching his old gags from the Jimmy Stewart picture. He told me when he started that he didn't want to do the same picture again, but instead, improve on his earlier material. George seemed to bubble over with comic invention.

"The studio insisted that I use a contract player in the Marlene Dietrich role. Mari Blanchard was the only girl on the lot who seemed to have any of the Dietrich quality that we wanted to recapture. She was also short; the right size to play opposite Murphy. However, we deliberately gave her character a new name and different songs to sing in order to get away, as much as possible, from an identification with Marlene, that was, of course, inevitable."

Mort Abrahams and Herb Ross

(Associate Producer and Director of the
1969 musical version of *Goodbye, Mr. Chips*)

Abrahams: "The addition of music and the required length of the picture forced us to make certain changes in the story. The most logical place to add material was in the relationship between Chips (Peter O'Toole) and his wife (Petula Clark). Otherwise, the musical sections of the film would have too many male voices.

---

1 James Stewart had starred with Marlene Dietrich in the 1939 version, directed by George Marshall.

"Almost none of us liked the idea of utilizing flashbacks, as we all felt it was a clumsy device. We also updated the story to involve the Second, instead of the First, World War.

"In retrospect, I don't think that the story lent itself to a road show production. We were forced to create new material that, simply, didn't work. And, of course, we were unfavorably compared to the original film. I think we'd have been much better off if the picture had only been two hours long."

Ross: "I entered the project late and had very little to do with the script or the score, which I felt was weak, though better than the one that the Previns had written.[2]

"I think that the major mistake was made by *not* using flashbacks. Had we gone with this device, we would have gotten a much better feeling of the passage of so many years and the generations of students. Flashbacks would have allowed us to jump around in the story by utilizing subjective recall, rather than straight narrative."

Ross: "Screenplays, especially those of the thirties and forties, have not dated as well as stage plays written during the same period. Dialogue in a top movie script just doesn't seem to match the often-timeless quality in the words of a good play.

"A beautiful example – *Double Indemnity* was a tremendous success when it was filmed in the forties. But, when it was re-done for television some time back, it was a flop and the reason was that they didn't update the dialogue. Instead, they used the original script almost word for word."

---

2 Andre' and Dore Previn had written the original score for the project and Gower Champion was hired as director. Later, when the trio withdrew over "artistic differences," Leslie Bricusse wrote a fresh score, John Williams became the new musical director and Ross was signed to direct.

Henry Blanke

(Producer/Associate Producer of *Four Daughters,* *The Maltese Falcon, Young at Heart*)

"Never remake a picture that was previously successful. Remake one that was miscast, miswritten, or misdirected. In other words, a flop.

"Otherwise you are competing with the audience's memory of the original picture."

"Unfortunately, I got stuck with Frank Sinatra for *Young at Heart.*[3]

"Warner Bros. wanted to do a picture with Sinatra, and Frank wanted to play the John Garfield part in a musical remake of *Four Daughters.*

"Garfield had died at the end of *Four Daughters.*

"'I'm a leading man,' Sinatra said. 'I don't die.'

"Frank didn't die in our picture, but we did eliminate one daughter from the story to make room for the songs."

"John Huston's film was the third film version of *The Maltese Falcon.*[4] I had produced the second version, *Satan Met a Lady* (1936) with Bette Davis and Warren William.

"It was the worst picture I ever made. Jack Warner ribbed me about it for years afterward. We only did it because Davis was under contract and the studio needed something for her to do.

"We decided that we could redo the story so soon after the original by switching certain elements around and turning the whole thing into a comedy.[5] But, as I later found out, the director, William Dieterle, had no flair for that kind of film and it failed."

"When John Huston was given the opportunity to direct his first film,

3 Doris Day co-starred in the 1954 remake, which was directed by Gordon Douglas.

4 The original version was released in 1931 and starred Ricardo Cortez (as Sam Spade) and Bebe Daniels.

5 The black falcon became a horn filled with precious gems and the Casper Gutman character, played by Sydney Greenstreet in the John Huston version, was rewritten for a woman (Alison Skipworth).

he wanted to do *The Maltese Falcon* and the fact that it had been done twice before didn't bother him.

"He followed the book exactly. He took two copies of it, cut them up to give him something to work from, then based his screenplay on what Dashiell Hammett had already written. Much of the dialogue from the film came directly from the novel.

"Four weeks after he began, Huston came to me with the thing all finished. I told him to stick the manuscript in a drawer and go fishing for eight weeks, since no studio head would have much faith in a screenplay that was written in such a short period of time.

"Our first choice to play Sam Spade was George Raft, but he refused to work with a first time director, so I cast Humphrey Bogart and he became a leading man."

Edward Dmytryk

(Director of the 1959 remake of *The Blue Angel*)

"I, initially, didn't want to do the picture, but agreed to do it in order to finish off my Fox contract. I enjoyed making it. We shot exteriors in Bavaria and the interiors back in Hollywood.

"I never considered the 1930 original with Marlene Dietrich and Emil Jannings[6] to be that much of a classic. That is, I don't think it's in the same league with, say... a *Stagecoach*. Dietrich was fine, but I think Jannings performance was rather 'hammy' by today's standards. Jurgens was much better.

"We stuck very close to the original story, because if you're going to do a remake, there's not much you can or should do to change it.

"We did, however, make some changes from the original. Unlike with Jannings, we felt there was no valid reason for Jurgens to die at the end. He suffers enough without dying and is, in a sense, an even more tragic figure alive. He's alive, but will never regain his former position.

---

6 In the remake, May Britt and Curt Jurgens played the roles originated by Dietrich and Jannings.

"Our film was also not as dreary or depraved as the original. We brought it up to date without changing the tack too much; the changes were in shading. Less emphasis on class distinction; and Jurgens, while of middle age, was not as old as Jannings made the character. Too, there are *attractive* girls in nightclubs these days; it was all on a somewhat higher level.

Director Edward Dmytryk, Mrs. Dmytryk
(actress Jean Porter) and the author

"Our major problem was that we didn't have Dietrich. I had originally brought May Britt to Fox for *The Young Lions*. She was inexperienced, but good for that role.

"May tried very hard on *The Blue Angel*, but was out of her depth. She wasn't a powerful enough personality to carry the film. I'd like to have had somebody else for the role, but there wasn't anyone.

"It's 'dangerous' to remake a classic . . . even a second-rate one like *The Blue Angel*."

John Lee Mahin

(Screenwriter of *Red Dust* and *Mogambo*)

"*Red Dust* (1932) was based on a stage play by William Collison. The original gave me just the bare beginnings of my screenplay. It was a heavy, turgid drama; nothing like we finally wound up with.

"Clark Gable was not the original choice for the leading role of 'Dennis Carson'. John Gilbert was supposed to do that part until I saw Clark in *Night Nurse* and suggested him for the role."

"The original picture was set in Indochina, but in 1952 Sam Zimbalist called me into his office at MGM and said: 'Let's do *Red Dust* in Africa.[7] We'll go on safari, do some gorillas and generally update the thing. It'll be fun.'

"I was enthusiastic about the project. It gave me the opportunity to fix my mistakes; to polish what I'd done on the first version. Actually, I think the story worked better in this new situation than in the 1932 film.

"In the original, Jean Harlow was a 'prostitute,' but in *Mogambo*, Ava Gardner played a not-too-bright showgirl with a tragic past.

"I wouldn't have done the remake without Gable."

George Sidney

(Director of the 1948 version of *The Three Musketeers*)

"*The Three Musketeers* is *not* a classic. Dumas was a popular writer of his time; the Irving Wallace of his day. He ran a 'writing factory'.

"I wanted to make a Western musical with swords and feather hats; a good action picture.

"We used the old sets from *A Tale of Two Cities* and shot part of the film on a golf course.

"We had to tone down the book. Censorship affected June Allyson's character and Gene Kelly's 'affair' with Lana Turner.

"Good material is so short today that they remake anything."

7 Zimbalist had produced the highly successful *King Solomon's Mines* in Africa.

Claire Trevor and John Carradine

(Actors in the 1939 version of *Stagecoch*)

Gordon Douglas, Martin Rackin, Bob Cummings and Stephanie Powers[8]

(Director, Producer and Actors for the 1966 remake)

Claire Trevor: "*Stagecoach* was the only thing I've ever done that couldn't have been done in another medium. It used the motion picture camera and music, folk songs with symphonic arrangements, that, up to that time, had never been done before.

"It should never have been remade. The remake 'missed the boat'.

John Carradine: "They deserved to lose their shirts on the remake. Nobody could have been better than John Wayne, Berton Churchill, Thomas Mitchell or me.

"Great classics should never be remade."

Gordon Douglas: "Frankly, the story wasn't strong enough to be remade. Also, in many areas the casting was weak. In the original, Claire Trevor looked like life had passed her by, but in our film, Ann-Margret didn't look like a hooker. And Alex Cord: Well, recasting John Wayne is a hard thing to do.

"We shot it outside of Denver, rather than in Monument Valley, because it was a better financial deal."[9]

8 In the 1966 film, Bob Cummings played the role of the crooked banker that had been originated by Berton Churchill and Stephanie Powers played Louise Platt's character, the pregnant wife of a cavalry officer.

9 John Ford had filmed the original 1939 *Stagecoach* in Monument Valley.

Martin Rackin: "Fox wanted to use James Coburn as 'Ringo,' but I wanted a new face, so we went with Alex Cord. I didn't feel that 'Ringo' should be played as naive as Wayne had done him. We updated the attitudes; went into the relationships more.

"In the original, they never stopped the coach during the Indian fight. We turned it over because it was more exciting and more believable.

"If I were to do it again, I'd change the title; call it *Ringo,* anything but *Stagecoach.* We were fighting the memory of a film that didn't really exist.

"There are just so many dramatic situations: *Stagecoach* has been made dozens of times: *The High and the Mighty... Airport... The Poseiden Adventure* – all of them were about a group of people caught in a tense situation. John Ford's film just came early enough to be considered innovative."

Bob Cummings: "The original *Stagecoach* was made when sound and good photography were new.

"They built up my part of the crooked banker; gave it a beginning and an ending.

"The picture taught me not to do roles that went against my image.

'If you watch the 1939 and our version together, you'll enjoy the new version better."

Stephanie Powers: "It's hard to remake things. Everybody had good intentions when they started, but the concept of the story is, by now, overdone.

"Everybody tried to do justice to the original."

W.R. Burnett

(Screenwriter of *High Sierra* and *I Died a Thousand Times*)

Raoul Walsh

(Director of *High Sierra* and *Colorado Territory*)

Burnett: "There was no real factual basis for *High Sierra* (1941), but it was inspired by John Dillinger.

"Paul Muni and George Raft both turned down the project, so we went with Humphrey Bogart, which was lucky for us."

Walsh: "Warners needed a picture to fill out their release schedule. I didn't have a project I was interested in at the time and there were no scripts 'on the shelf' that I liked. So, I suggested that we change *High Sierra* to a Western format.[10] It was a relatively easy task and we found that we could shoot the picture very quickly."

Burnett: "It was Jack Warner's idea to remake *High Sierra*. It was supposed to be a vehicle for Frank Sinatra, but when he demanded fifty percent of the box-office net, they hired Jack Palance on a straight salary.[11]

"I toned down some of the sentimental aspects in the script, as I felt that Mark Hellinger, who'd produced the first version, had gone a bit overboard in this area. But, otherwise, the only thing I really did was to tighten up what I'd previously written.

---

10 Joel McCrea inherited the Bogart role and Virginia Mayo played the Ida Lupino character in the 1949 Western, titled *Colorado Territory*.

11 Stuart Heisler directed the CinemaScope/WarnerColor production, *I Died a Thousand Times*, with Palance and Shelley Winters in the Bogart and Lupino roles. Lee Marvin was also in the cast, playing a member of Palance's gang.

" I felt the casting was wrong. Palance was too much of a villain to be as sympathetic as Bogie was."

Allan Jones

(Played "Ravenal" the 1936 film version of *Show Boat*)

John Lee Mahin, George Sidney and Howard Keel

(Screenwriter, Director and Star ("Ravenal")
of the 1951 version of *Show Boat*)

Jones: "Most of the cast had done the play before. In fact, Charles Winninger ("Captain Andy") and Helen Morgan ("Julie") were in the original New York company. Universal borrowed me from MGM to play "Ravenal."

"I think that our picture was the best of the three[12]. We may not have had color like the 1951 version did, but director James Whale certainly created a realistic Southern atmosphere. Natchez really looked like a town of that period – not something that was on a studio backlot.

"Kern and Hammerstein wrote 'I Have the Room Above Her,' a new song for me to sing in the picture."

Mahin: "My long contract at MGM had expired, but Arthur Freed asked me to come back and do this script. I'd always thought that 'Julie' was the best part in the story. Arthur agreed and we decided that the role should be built-up. For example, in our film, 'Ravenal' (Howard Keel) goes back to 'Magnolia' (Kathryn Grayson) as a direct result of an accidental encounter with 'Julie' (Ava Gardner), who informs him that he has a daughter.

12 The first filming of *Show Boat* had been released by Universal in 1929 with Joseph Schildkraut in the role of "Ravenal.""

"I also thought it was wrong to keep the lovers apart for such a long period of time, so I reunited them on the showboat after about five years."

Sidney: "MGM didn't want to buy *Show Boat* from Universal. But, back in 1938, there were two other stories that Metro wanted from that studio and they were forced to take the Kern/Hammerstein musical as part of a package. The property lay around for years until Arthur Freed decided he wanted to do it.

"We did very little to the play – just streamlined the main incidents somewhat and freshened the dialogue."

Keel: "I didn't really want to do the film because I always thought 'Ravenal' was rather bland – a bit of a shnook. But, I must admit that the writer, John Mahin, *did* get into the character and made him more interesting."

Henry Blanke and Ida Lupino

(Associate Producer and star of the 1941 version of *The Sea Wolf*)

William Sackheim, Ruth Roman and Dane Clark

(Screenwriter and stars of *Barricade*)

Lindsley Parsons

(Producer of *Wolf Larsen*)

Blanke: "*The Sea Wolf* was supposed to be a vehicle for Paul Muni, but when he turned it down, we cast Edward G. Robinson as 'Wolf Larsen."

"One day, Jack Warner came across a magazine item that said Jack London wrote *The Sea Wolf* within a two week period. He showed me the clipping and asked, 'If London could do it in that short of time, why can't our writer, Robert Rossen?' He was only *half*-serious."

Lupino: "It was considered a prestige production and I enjoyed working with John Garfield.

"John and I almost drowned in one scene. Our director (Michael Curtiz) didn't tell us that this huge amount of water was going to come down this chute and hit us.

`He didn't tell a lot of people because several crew members were injured."

Sackheim: "Saul Elkins had a low budget production unit on the Warner lot, and it was his idea to turn *The Sea Wolf* into a Western. I was assigned to adapt the Rossen script. They ran the Robinson film for me, and then they announced that the project would be titled *Barricade.*

"To this day, I have no idea what that title meant.

"Our most difficult problem was in isolating the characters so there could be no escape from the rule of our 'Wolf Larsen'. Naturally, that kind of isolation is easier to come by on a boat, but I solved the problem by making our 'captain' the owner of a gold mine that utilized slave labor. Raymond Massey played the role, renamed 'Boss' Kruger in the 1950 release."

Roman: "I wasn't aware that it was a remake at the time we made it.

"Dane Clark really got shot in that film. He zigged when he should have zagged."

Clark: "I was sick about it. It was an ugly experience; a 'B' picture. I'd just come off suspension at the time and the studio assigned me to this as punishment.

"I was also supposed to do the remake of *The Jazz Singer,* but they took it away from me when I refused to re-sign for seven years."[13]

Parsons: "Sterling Hayden brought the *Wolf Larsen* project to me, but the way *he* wanted to film it would have been too expensive. He thought we should take his boat out and play the sea sequences for real. That is, shoot film in actual storms and so forth. That would have been fine, however our two hundred thousand dollar budget made 'faking' these sequences mandatory.

"Hayden didn't want to compromise his vision, so he withdrew from the project, but he did let us use his hundred-foot schooner, the *Gracie S,* for the ten day shoot."[14]

Howard Hawks

(Director of *Rio Bravo, El Dorado, Rio Lobo*[15])

"I did *Rio Bravo* because I was asked to give my opinion of *High Noon,* which I didn't like. A good sheriff would have kept the incapable townsfolk out of the fight, but in *High Noon,* Gary Cooper tried to get the citizens to join him. John Wayne didn't do that."

13 Danny Thomas would star in the 1953 remake of *The Jazz Singer.*

14 Barry Sullivan replaced Hayden in the title role in *Wolf Larsen,* released in 1958.

15 To various degrees, *El Dorado* (1966) and *Rio Lobo* (1970) were partial remakes of *Rio Bravo* (1959). All three films starred John Wayne.

"I don't consider the second two films remakes. Similar characters were used with variations. They were good characters.

"I often repeat a scene that I thought was good."

"*El Dorado* had a finished script based on a book. I didn't like it. I kept the opening parts, then I looked at the notes from *Rio Bravo* and took elements we hadn't used."

"I found Walter Brennan when he was an extra. He never needed to know the story before he signed with me."

"Wayne said: 'Next time, can I play the drunk?'."[16]

"I believe in making good scenes. I don't care that much about story."

16 In *Rio Bravo,* Dean Martin played John Wayne's drunken deputy sheriff and, in *El Dorado,* Robert Mitchum, essentially, played the same role.

One Good Film Deserves Another

Writing a book about movie sequels seemed like a natural follow-up to Make It Again, Sam, *my book about film remakes. Luckily,* One Good Film Deserves Another *was published in 1977, before Hollywood's practice of producing sequels to successful movies exploded. Indeed, if I were to update this book today, the study would probably take up volumes.*

Whether they'd actually made a sequel or not, here is what some of Hollywood's successful filmmakers had to say about the practice of making sequels:

Stanley Rubin

(Producer of *River of No Return,*
The President's Analyst, Francis in the Navy)

"If a sequel is going to be truly successful, it must explore the plot and characters of the original with more depth. Sometimes it's difficult, if not impossible, to expand on a story.

"Doing the *Francis* picture was more like working on a television series than a feature film. The characters didn't grow and you had to find new locales and different ways to tell the same jokes about a talking mule."

Herb Ross

(Director of *The Sunshine Boys, Funny Lady*)

"The main problem with sequels is one of integrity. One must be very conscious of not doing a 'rip-off'. Intentions should be serious and proper time and money spent."

Stirling Silliphant

(Screenwriter of *In the Heat of the Night, Charly*)

"Many movies don't lend themselves toward sequelization, but those that do should be studied carefully by the makers of the follow-up, so they can spot and evaluate the mistakes, thereby coming up with a better picture."

Dore Schary

(Screenwriter of *Young Tom Edison* and *Edison, the Man*)

"John Considine, the producer, originally wanted to do one long picture honoring Edison. Mickey Rooney would play the boy, then we'd *dissolve* and Spencer Tracy would be the adult. It didn't take us long to realize that such an optical effect would produce the biggest laugh in the history of movies, so we decided to divide the project in half."

Edwin Blum

(Screenwriter of *Down to Earth* [1947], sequel to *Here Comes Mr. Jordan*[1])

"I came up with an original story, *A Guy and a Goddess*, which dealt with Terpscihore, the muse of song and dance and her visit to the world of mortals.

"It took me five years to develop this supernatural musical. Part of the delay came about when *One Touch of Venus* opened on Broadway. I had to rethink my story so that people wouldn't accuse me of stealing material from that show.

"Finally, after deciding that my Terpscihore would come down from the

1 Alexander Hall directed the classic 1941 fantasy from Columbia Pictures. It starred Robert Montgomery, Evelyn Keyes, Claude Rains, James Gleason and Edward Everett Horton.

Heavens to enact herself in a play, I took the project to Harry Cohn at Columbia and suggested he cast Rita Hayworth as the goddess. When I mentioned muses, Cohn lost his temper (he was always firing me) and practically threw me out of his office. 'If you think that Rita Hayworth will play a Greek,' he yelled, 'you're crazy'.

"A year of so went by. I was playing tennis with writer/producer Don Hartman and he asked me if I had a story that would be right for Rita Hayworth. I told him about *A Guy and a Goddess.* He liked it, called Harry Cohn on the phone, and Cohn said for him to bring me right over.

"In the meantime, I'd called my agent and asked him what to do. After all, I'd already told Cohn this story and he'd refused it. But my agent said not to worry – that Cohn wouldn't remember the plot.

"Actually, I think he remembered it in his subconscious thoughts, because as I related the story to him, which I hadn't reread for some time, he would fill in small details that I'd forgotten. Yet, he didn't recall that I'd told it to him before.

"Cohn liked the story and we made a deal for me to co-author the screenplay with Hartman. But, there was one major element missing from the plot: How would Terpscihore arrive on earth to become a temporary mortal?

"'We'll bring back Mr. Jordan,' Cohn said. 'He'll be the halfway point between Mt. Parnassus and Broadway'.[2] And, that's what we did.

"I wasn't too happy with some of the film's casting. I'd always wanted Rita Hayworth for the movie. In fact, the story was written with her in mind. But, I thought that Gene Kelly would have been a better choice for the male lead. Musically, he was far more talented than Larry Parks who, in my opinion, could only mimic Al Jolson."

---

2 Roland Culver replaced Claude Rains as Mr. Jordan in *Down to Earth,* but James Gleason and Edward Everett Horton reprised their roles from the original film.

William Alland

(Producer of *The Creature From the Black Lagoon* trilogy)

"I really got involved in the first *Creature* movie, but the last two were just 'spit-out.'"

George Sherman

(Director of *Against All Flags, The Battle of Apache Pass, Big Jake*)

"Sequels are generally never as good as the original picture. Producers and directors work so hard trying to improve on the original that they overshoot the field. They overdo it and the picture lacks spontaneity. Actors think they're aping previous actors.

"It's like telling a joke twice. It's not as fresh the second time."

Philip D'Antoni

(Producer of *The French Connection*)

"Immediately after *The French Connection* came out, Fox came to me and told me to make a sequel. I agreed to work on the script because I had a percentage of the new project, but I didn't promise to produce it because I was too involved then with *The Seven-Ups,* which I was going to also direct.[3]

"I also felt I had already done the ultimate *French Connection.* However, I did have a momentary regret when I saw *The Godfather II.*"

3 Robert L. Rosen would produce *French Connection II.*

Charlton Heston

Charlton Heston

Charlton Heston *(1976) was a book I wrote for a series, entitled* Pyramid Illustrated History of the Movies. *I had never really been a Heston fan, but for the work involved, it was a well-paying assignment, so I took the job.*

Interestingly, the editor of the series instructed me not *to interview the actor, but to concentrate on his films. This, in short, was to be an extended filmography, rather than an in-depth biography.*

*Nevertheless, in researching my book, I did speak to a few people who had worked with Heston, including Tom Gries, who directed him in several films (*Will Penny, The Hawaiians *and* Number One*). I also talked to Jessica Walter and Christopher Mitchum, both former publicity clients of mine who had worked with Heston. Jessica played his wife in* Number One *and Mitchum had a key role in* The Last Hard Men.

If Heston ever read my book, I'm sure he was not happy with it, because I did give my opinion of his work as an actor. It certainly wasn't brutal, but it was honest.

That's why, years later, when I was directing my screenplay of The Doorway *in Ireland for producer Roger Corman and I was offered Heston as my five-day star,*[1] *I opted instead for Roy Scheider.*

Yes, Heston was a slightly bigger name and an Oscar winner, but Scheider was the better actor. Also, if Heston had *read my book and remembered it, that could have caused me problems during filming.*

Incidentally, I had a great time working with Roy Scheider.

---

1 A low budget picture, particularly one made by Roger Corman, is usually cast with unknown actors, but to enhance the film's appeal, a well-known performer is hired for less than their usual fee to play a key role that can be shot out in a maximum of five days.

Tom Gries

"Directors are shy when working with stars of large physical stature. On *Will Penny,* I told Heston to play smaller than life. Penny was a frightened man."

"Heston has bad acting habits; weaknesses. He has a tendency to play the emotional end of a scene before he gets there, and he grimaces. He is not a very relaxed man.

"I stood behind the camera and called his attention to it."

"On *The Hawaiians,* he was back to grimacing. I was annoyed with him, because he was preparing to direct his film version of *Anthony and Cleopatra,* and his mind was on that."

"He developed *Number One.* He wanted to do a film where he wasn't the largest man on screen."

Jessica Walter

"He was one of the most professional, super gentlemen I've ever worked with. When I met him, I thought I really was meeting Moses. He really was that handsome; that overwhelming."

"I never saw him look in the mirror once."

Christopher Mitchum

"Chuck is one hell of a man. The first thing that impressed me about him was acting with him. He plays you eye-to-eye; gives all he can, and never tries to take from you during a scene the way many major – or minor, for that matter – actors do. This fits in with his entire being, which, if I had to describe in one word, is 'sincere.' He is a very genuine person."

"I'm a chess player as victims such as John Wayne will tell you.

"Chuck plays chess, so while we were filming *The Last Hard Men,* we started playing. I beat him, and I beat him some more. On one trip home during filming, he brought back his own pieces; said that he was just wasn't used to the other pieces. I beat him some more.

"Then, I started giving him some lessons. I would spot him a piece, my queen at first, and then help him with theory as we played the game. He improved quickly. Soon, I would no longer spot him a piece and he would be sure of winning. Still, with all the pieces on the board, I beat him.

"Finally, he announced that the pieces were too small. He couldn't see them well enough. If only they were larger, he could beat me.

"On a weekend trip to Mexico, I bought him a giant chess board. The pieces were five inches tall and the board about thirty inches on a side. I gave it to Chuck at lunch with a note, saying 'If this is too small, you take the Americas ….'

"Several days later, we played on the large board. Chuck won.

"I must say that he took winning very well. When the film was over, he presented me with an 8x10 picture of himself bent over a chessboard. Written in his hand in a comic balloon over his head was: '… Now, if I just move Mitchum's rook over two squares before he gets back ….'"

Robert Clary, Merv Griffin, the author and comic Milt Kamens

Merv

Because he was more of a television personality than a movie star, I hadn't planned to include anything from Merv, *my 1976 biography of talk show host Merv Griffin, in this volume, but then I remembered a trio of choice stories he told me, which I will now share with you.*

This was a fun book to write, since Merv was extremely cooperative, spending many interview hours with me and giving me access to the people in his life, past and present. After Award Books published the paperback in 1976, he brought me onto his show to promote it.

In 1980, Leisure Books published an updated edition.

Growing up, Merv's favorite movie star was Errol Flynn and when he was sixteen years old, he got the opportunity to meet the screen's "Captain Blood," a friend of his Uncle Elmer. Whenever the screen's leading swashbuckler was between marriages, he would board with Elmer, who had founded the West Side Tennis Club in Los Angeles.

Merv's family lived in the San Francisco area, but on this particular summer vacation, the young naïve man was invited to spend some time with his uncle.

"I arrived at Elmer's house," Merv recalled, "and I was shocked to see Flynn standing in the living room – stark naked.

"I was dumbfounded. I didn't know what to say. Here was my idol, and the first time I met him, he was in the raw with a drink in his hand.

"But what really threw me is when these beautiful ladies would come over, and he still wouldn't put any clothes on.

A few days after I arrived, I got a phone call from my mother. She wanted to know if I was enjoying myself. 'I'm having a lot of fun, Mom,' I said. 'And guess what! Errol Flynn is staying with us.'

"There was a brief silence at the other end of the line, followed by a very quiet, but firm, 'Let me speak to your uncle.'

"Elmer got on the phone and did calm his sister-in-law down with 'Don't worry. The boy's fine' and all that.

"Then, I got back on the line, and finished the conversation with: 'Everything's great, Mom. They send me to the movies every day.'"

During the early 1950s, Merv was a contract player at Warner Brothers, but none of the roles he was given to play amounted to much. "I had thought it would be fun to be a movie star," he said. "I didn't know you had to act. I missed the audience – getting a reaction after I finished[1] – and was, frankly, bored.

"They cast me in a Western, *The Boy From Oklahoma* (1954) with Will Rogers, Jr. He was the sheriff and I was playing his deputy. Michael Curtiz was the director.

"I had never been on a horse before, and Curtiz promised me two weeks of instruction before we began filming. But, he double-crossed me.

"I was called to the set on the first day of shooting and told to *lead* a fifty-man posse – all experienced riders – down a hill. My protests fell on deaf ears.

"There I was coming down the hill at a gallop, holding the reins with one hand, and frantically keeping my hat from slipping off with the other. Suddenly, I realized the posse had passed me.

"Curtiz yelled 'Cut!', then looked at me and said, "Greefing, you stink on de lousy horse!'

"All through the picture it was the same way. I'd fall off my horse, my hat kept slipping down over my eyes, and I blinked every time I shot my gun.

1 Prior to signing with the studio, Griffin had been a singer with the Freddy Martin Orchestra.

"In one scene, I decided to have some fun, and after making my scripted announcement (*"Come on, everybody! Clear the street for the horse race."*), I did an impression (physically only) of Jackie Gleason's famous 'Away we go' exit. Curtiz, who didn't watch Gleason's show and, therefore, was unaware of why the cast and crew were laughing, decided to leave this 1954 gag in the 1800s Western.

"*The Boy From Oklahoma* soured me on making pictures. I became camera shy and started to duck the studio casting office. Whenever they would call, I used to answer the telephone in my Chinese voice. I'd say, 'Mastah Griffin not here. He in San Diego'.

"We once thought it might be funny to devote one of the talk shows to a 'Merv Griffin Film Festival,' yet, after we looked at all the clips, we realized that the whole thing would last four minutes."

After he left Warner Brothers, Merv was selected by the legendry Tallulah Bankhead as her opening act at the Sands Hotel in Las Vegas. He would never forget that engagement's closing night.

"At the party, Tallulah ordered a zombie and so did I. It was like fruit punch. Nothing happened. So, we changed to daiquiris. We were both dead drunk and dead drunk we played blackjack – which was strictly against the house rules at the Sands. Entertainers appearing there were not allowed to gamble at the hotel's casino.

"We stayed at the table all night, and by ten the next morning – with guests in their bathing suits gathered around to watch – I'd won twelve thousand, and Tallulah had eight.

'Jack Entratter, entertainment director and part owner of the hotel, came over – and he was angry. He took both of us firmly by the arms, cashed in our chips, and led us upstairs while the crowd watched in stunned silence – waiting for Tallulah's exit line, which everyone knew was inevitable.

"Halfway up the stairs, she turned back to the public and said, 'Well, isn't anyone going to fuck me tonight, dahling?'

"Everybody broke up – including Entratter."

The Musical

From Broadway to Hollywood

The Musical: From Broadway to Hollywood *was the last of five books that I wrote for A.S. Barnes & Company. It's also the only book in that quintet for which my interview notes seem to have disappeared.*

Nevertheless, I have pulled a few quotes from the body of the book itself, which you will, hopefully, find interesting.

The purpose of this 1980 work was to trace the journey a Broadway musical makes from the theatre to the motion picture screen and why changes are made by filmmakers during its travels.

*Among the people I interviewed were composer Jule Styne (*Gentlemen Prefer Blondes, Gypsy, Funny Girl*); Paul Francis Webster (three-time Oscar-winning lyricist, including "Secret Love" from* Calamity Jane*); producer Sol C. Siegel (*Gentlemen Prefer Blondes*); screenwriter William Ludwig (*Oklahoma!*); screenwriter and co-director (with Stanley Donen) George Abbott and composer/lyricist (with Jerry Ross) Richard Adler of* Damn Yankees*; director Mervyn LeRoy (*Gypsy*); music supervisor John Green and actress Shani Wallis (*Oliver!*); and director Arthur Hiller (*Man of La Mancha*).*

Jule Styne

"Today, when one of my shows is sold to movies, part of the deal states that any interpolation[1] must be done by myself. That was the case when we sold *Funny Girl*. Bob Merrill, the lyricist, and I wrote a special title song for the picture."

Paul Francis Webster, the author and composer Sammy Fain

Paul Francis Webster

"I was hired to update the lyrics for the MGM productions of *The Student Prince* (1954), *Rose Marie* (1954) and *The Merry Widow* (1952). The problem with this kind of lyric writing is that you have to make the songs contemporary enough so that they'll work today, but still retain about the same

1 i.e. making changes to an existing song and/or adding a new song to an existing play. For the film version of *Gentlemen Prefer Blondes*, Hoagy Carmichael and Harold Adamson had written new songs, rather than original Broadway composer, Styne, and his collaborator, Leo Robin.

mood and feeling as was in the original. In other words, you take out the archaic, yet are careful not to change so much that the people who love the work will resent what you've done. There are some cases, of course, in which you'll interpolate altogether new songs."

"I worked directly with composer Rudolf Friml on *Rose Marie.* "He wasn't too sensitive about lyric changes in general, except when it came to using the word 'kiss'. On that he was impossible. He was probably in his late seventies then and refused to work on songs with 'kiss' in them because, he claimed, since kissing transferred germs, it was unhygienic. We had to bring in a ghostwriter to finish the song."

Sol C. Siegel

"I'd seen *Gentlemen Prefer Blondes* in New York with Carol Channing and, although I found it entertaining, there was not much substance to the plot. It was too thin to work in a film. Broadway musicals, back then particularly, were notorious for their weak story lines.

"It was not a property I would have chosen for myself, but Darryl Zanuck asked me to do it as a favor."

"I never considered Betty Grable[2] to play 'Lorelei,' but there were conversations with Miss Channing. We wanted to test her, but her agent refused to let her test unless we gave her a Fox contract beforehand. On that basis, I refused and went with Marilyn Monroe, whom we already had under contract."

"Jack Cole did the choreography for the picture, but it was his assistant, Gwen Verdon, who walked Marilyn through the 'Diamonds Are a Girl's Best Friend' number."

2 At the time, Betty Grable was a top contract star at 20th Century Fox.

William Ludwig

"I don't think *Oklahoma!* was as good as it could have been. We weren't allowed the opportunity to break out of the proscenium and take full advantage of the camera.

"Rodgers and Hammerstein had complete control down to the last comma. You really couldn't argue with their success or their control. They wanted the film to be as close to their smash stage success as possible.

"Every time director Fred Zinnemann tried to open up a scene and use the camera, Hammerstein was there to pull him back. For example, Agnes deMille choreographed 'The Farmer and the Cowman' number exactly the way she'd done it on the stage twelve years before. When Fred argued that he wanted to utilize a large camera boom and play the number over the entire set, which filled two soundstages at Metro, he was overruled.

"The only number he was allowed to expand was "Kansas City," which we staged outside at the railroad depot and on top of a train."

"We tried to expand the character of Jud (Rod Steiger) – flesh him out a bit with short scenes that were not in the play – but these were eliminated before filming began."

"Another problem we had was with the play's repetitive lines. On stage, it might be necessary to repeat a fact two or three times in order to set up a gag. But, in movies, a close-up can make your point the first time.

"We wanted to cut some of the repetition, however Hammerstein wouldn't hear of it. He had a tremendous loose-leaf notebook with him that appeared to be a record of every performance of *Oklahoma!* If I suggested cutting such and such a line, he'd look in the book and say, 'Impossible! That line got a sixteen second laugh in Boston.' He wasn't about to sacrifice anything."

George Abbott & Richard Adler

Abbott: "I wanted my Broadway cast to repeat their roles in *Damn Yankees,* but Warner Bros. and good sense dictated that we use at least one movie name.

"Somebody suggested Marilyn Monroe for Gwen Verdon's role of 'Lola.' We had lunch with her one day. I doubt if she was really interested in the part. She was just pulling our legs."

Adler: "I don't believe that Marilyn could do the dancing the role required."

Abbott: "Warners put a lot of pressure on us to cast Tab Hunter, who was one of their contract players. It wasn't the best idea in the world, but we went along with it.

"Hollywood studios sometimes come up with unusual thoughts for casting. When we did *The Pajama Game* on film, they tried to get me to use Bing Crosby in the John Raitt role. He'd have been all wrong."

Adler: "On the surface, Tab Hunter as Joe Hardy was not such a bad suggestion. He had a face that was so handsome that it didn't look real. He could have been a composite man created by God ... or the devil."

Abbott: "The film could have been better. We tried different bits – like having the devil get dressed to a speeded-up camera – but many of these didn't work out."

Adler: "I wasn't too happy with the movie. It stayed too close to the play and didn't utilize the medium of film enough."

Mervyn LeRoy

"With *Gypsy,* I decided that we would deviate very little from the New York production. Why take a great show and improve it into a flop?"

"Ethel Merman is a great talent, and I love her. She, of course, was dying to play Mama Rose in the picture, but we had to turn her down. No matter how big a star she is on Broadway, her name means very little at the movie box office. *Gypsy* was going to be too important a project to gamble on anything less than a major film star with a proven track record.

"Ever since I'd first seen the play, I knew there was only one actress who could play the part, and that was Rosalind Russell."

John Green and Shani Wallis

Green: "With *Oliver!,* director Carol Reed wanted to go back to the essence of Charles Dickens. He began with the original novel, then worked up through the concept that Lionel Bart had employed in his play. On stage, *Oliver!* was done in a very stylized manner, but the movie opened up the show considerably and played it on a realistic level. At one point, Bart thought we were destroying his play.

"We had a fundamental difference in the *Oliver!* music. In the theatre, a fourteen-piece orchestra was used to give a chamber opera effect but, on film, we had a seventy-four piece symphony orchestra."

Wallis: "I was living in New York and went back and forth to Hollywood for various tests for almost a year before I knew I had the part of 'Nancy'.

"The producers kept experimenting. They dyed my red hair black – because Georgia's was black,[3] I guess – then had me go back to the original red."

Wallis: "Carol Reed was a marvelous director and a very stubborn man. Even though he'd never directed a musical before, he followed his instincts – which were usually right – rather than blindly following the well-meaning suggestions of those who were more experienced with musical productions

"He turned many musical situations around and took songs that were just 'sung' on stage and used them in a more dramatic sense. For example, in my 'Oom-Pah-Pah' number, he had me steal Oliver away from Sykes while I sang and danced. That sort of thing wasn't done on stage."

3 Georgia Brown had played "Nancy" in the London and New York stage productions.

Arthur Hiller

"Perhaps *Man of La Mancha* should never have been made into a film. It's one of those special pieces of theatre that works brilliantly on stage where reality is easily suspended, but suffers when placed before the cold eye of the movie camera."

"I was agreeable to the casting of Peter O'Toole and Sophia Loren or I wouldn't have joined the venture.[4] I chose Harry Andrews to play the Innkeeper. The sets caused me no particular problems and I altered them to suit my needs."

"The essential problem of transferring the play to film was that the play takes place in the mind's eye. We had to figure out a way to establish the prison-reality, the fantasy, and make the transitions between them."

4 Hiller replaced director Peter Glenville after Glenville's concept of the material conflicted with that of playwright/screenwriter Dale Wasserman.

The Hollywood Legends

Clark Gable

Gable

Gable *was written in 1983 and was the first play in* The Hollywood Legends *collection. It was first presented at the Stage Door Theatre in Agoura Hills, California, opening on February 2, 1984. My friend, actor Michael Ansara, directed that production, which starred Boyd Holister as "Clark Gable."*

Among the people I interviewed when researching the play were my former publicity client, Edward Dmytryk, who directed Gable in Soldier of Fortune, *and screenwriter John Lee Mahin, who wrote many Gable pictures, including* Test Pilot, Boom Town *and* Mogambo.

Here are some of the things they said to me:

Edward Dmytryk

"Gable could be a nasty drunk. I remember his getting loaded once and berating the film's publicist, who was just doing his job."

"My wife and I own the house in Bel Air that used to belong to Carole Lombard. There's an aviary in the back yard.

"Clark liked to tell about the time he and Carole got into an argument; she locked him in the aviary and turned on the sprinklers. He sat there for an hour.

"'That ought to cool you off,' she said."

The author, actor Boyd Holister and director Michael Ansara on the set of the initial production of *Gable.*

"'I'm a better actor than they think I am,' he said. And, he was."

"I couldn't shoot a long close-up of Clark.
After a couple of minutes, his head would start to
tremble every so slightly, and I'd have to call 'Cut!'."

John Lee Mahin

"Clark's father was a hard man. Even when Clark became a big star, his father considered acting to be 'sissy work'. But, Clark felt a duty toward his father, and in his wives, he was looking for a 'mother'."

"The first time he dated Kay,[1] he took her out to dinner, then brought her back to his house and suggested that she go upstairs and get undressed. She told him to go fuck himself."

"He knew that Spencer Tracy could act rings around him. 'If I go beyond a second take,' he said, 'he'll kill me and I'll be conscious of his taking charge.'"

"He didn't like working with Greer Garson. He felt she should work in period films."

"Yes, he did have an affair with Grace Kelly during *Mogambo*."

"When he was in the military, he was afraid of being ridiculed because he was a movie star, and also of being shot down over Germany. Before one rough mission, he asked me: 'Do you believe in Jesus... in God?' Then, he said, 'I believe in a good man in love with a good woman.'"

"When he first saw my script for *Mogambo*, he got mad at me. 'You son-of-a-bitch,' he said, 'you've given Ava (Gardner) all the funny lines.'

"'Yes,' I said, 'but the audience won't laugh until we cut to your reaction'.

"And, I was right."

1 Kay Spreckels was Gable's last wife.

Al Jolson

Jolson

My one person/one piano player stage play, Jolson, *began life after comedian and my former publicity client, Jack Carter, saw a performance of* Gable, *then hired me to write him a like play on Al Jolson.*

During the research phase of the project, Jack arranged for me to meet music director/composer Milton DeLugg, who had worked with Jolson during the filming of Jolson Sings Again *and, in fact, appears briefly on screen, playing his accordion. I also spoke to Erle, Jolson's widow, then married to playwright Norman Krasna, actress Betty Garrett, the widow of Larry Parks, who had played Jolson in the two biographical films, and comedian George Burns.*

Unfortunately, Carter and I had a falling out over the direction of the play and, in settling our contract; I assumed full ownership of the material. Over the next year, I cleared the song rights with the various music publishers.

The play had its debut in Los Angeles in 1987 and, since then, it has successfully played in many cities throughout the United States.

Without Jack Carter's participation in the beginning stages of Jolson, *I would probably not have had as easy access to some of the people I interviewed, and for that I am certainly grateful to him.*

Here are some things that those folks had to say about Al Jolson:

Milton DeLugg

"He used to refer to himself in the third person. He'd say things like 'Jolie likes you.' Or, in one instance: 'Jolie made a fartsola.'"

"Jolson had a cruel sense of humor. He told this story about a song plugger who was trying to sell him one of his songs. While the poor guy was standing there singing, Jolson stood next to him, pissing on his leg.

"'I bought the song,' he said, 'but I didn't put my name on it.'

"Jolson put his name on a few songs that he didn't actually write."

"He was not flexible with the beat or tempo of his songs."

"Jolson 'stabbed' Jessel in the back on *The Jazz Singer*.[1]He went around Jessel and talked Jack Warner into letting him star in the movie version, which was the first talking picture.

"I think he was 'paranoid' about Jessel. Unlike Al, George was bright; a legitimate actor, and Jolson felt inferior to him."

"Jolson admired Ezio Pinza.[2]
He spent his spare time rehearsing his songs."

"I think Jolson was afraid of his feelings."

1 George Jessel had starred in the Broadway production of *The Jazz Singer*.

2 Pinza starred with Mary Martin in the Broadway production of *South Pacific*. Songs he introduced include "Some Enchanted Evening."

Mrs. Erle Krasna

"Al had a temper. He'd scream, but then the temper was gone.

"He was also a terrible driver. Once a cop stopped him and Al lost his temper. He didn't get a ticket because the cop was a fan."

"He was a loner. He read a lot; saw every movie. We went out every night, but to sporting events or movies; not to parties."

"He was never *legally* married to Ethel,[3] but he continued to support her after she went into an institution."

"He once knocked a pianist off a piano stool when he played the wrong notes."

"Al wasn't happy with Larry Parks playing him in *The Jolson Story*. He said: 'He can't move from the waist down.'"

"Al didn't want George Jessel to deliver his eulogy. He said: 'Jessel will give my eulogy, and the next day he'll call my widow for a date.'"[4]

---

3 Ethel Delmar was Jolson's second wife.

4 George Jessel delivered Jolson's eulogy.

Betty Garrett

"Jolson was antagonistic. He ignored Larry."

"He attempted to show Larry how to do a number, but when Larry tried it, he said: 'You're doing too much.'

"Jolson was unaware of how much he overdid. He always sang at top energy, It was hard to fit his song performances into a picture performance."

"Jolson wanted Jimmy Cagney or Richard Conte to play him"

"He hung around the set and bugged people."

George Burns

"When he was not on stage, Al would run water in his dressing room, so that he couldn't hear the people on stage getting applause."

"For years at Hillcrest (Country Club), he spent $200 per week to have sturgeon flown in special for him from New York."

"Sometimes he would sit in the box-office, and if a customer asked the location of a seat, he wouldn't sell them a ticket."

"When Gracie and I had a party at our house, guests would get up and sing a song. I had a hard and fast rule: one song per customer.

"Al did his number, got terrific applause, and then started to do another song. I reminded him: 'one song per customer,' and then I started to do my number, 'Red Rose Rag'.

"He got angry and stormed out of the house.
I followed him out, still singing.

"He got into his car and realized that he'd forgotten his wife's mink coat. He came back to get it, and I was still singing."

Errol Flynn as Robin Hood

Flynn

Written in 1984, Flynn *is one of the few one-person plays in* The Hollywood Legends *collection that has never had a production.*

There have been some false starts; a couple of stage productions in Los Angeles that didn't go beyond the first couple weeks of rehearsal, as well as an aborted audio production.

I think that the problem is that Errol Flynn is not an easy character to portray, and the fact that my play requires the actor playing the part to move back-and-forth between the swashbuckler's younger days and the end of his life (at age fifty) doesn't help matters.

Nevertheless, the script is a fun read and, hopefully, one of these days an actor who can pull it off will present himself.

Among the people I interviewed when researching the play were director George Sherman, a former publicity client, who directed Flynn and Maureen O'Hara in Against All Flags *(1952), and the actor's second wife, Nora Eddington. They met when she was eighteen; working at the snack counter in the Los Angeles courthouse during the time that Flynn was on trial for rape. They were married from 1943 to 1948 and had two children. After they were divorced, she married singer Dick Haymes, but that union also ended in divorce in 1953.*

Nora had a small role in Flynn's Adventures of Don Juan *(1948).*

George Sherman

"The first thing that Errol said to me on the set was: 'I go home at five-thirty.'

"'You'll be lonely,' I said. 'I go home at four-thirty.'"

"Errol would sit in his dressing room drinking
straight vodka, but he never blew a line."

"Once he said to Maureen O'Hara: 'I'm so sorry I'm late. You are the cause I couldn't sleep all night long. You are the most beautiful woman on screen. I've looked forward to working with you.'"

"He said: 'They treated me like a dog at Warner Brothers.'"

Nora Eddington

"His mother was unfaithful to his father,
and Errol adored his father."

"He was heavy into drugs after 1945-46. He tried pot, opium, and morphine. Narcotics ruined our marriage. He beat me up."

"Errol wasn't anti-Semitic, but he
kidded about being anti-Semitic."

"He preferred the company of men, rather than women."

❧

"I caught Errol twice fooling around, and that was the end of it. I said to him: 'If you hadn't thrown it in my face, it would've been more acceptable.'"

❧

"Errol didn't want the divorce, but I was involved with Dick Haymes already."

Clara Bow

Clara Bow

Silent film star Clara Bow was the movies' first American sex goddess, the forerunner to Jean Harlow, Rita Hayworth and Marilyn Monroe.

Although my one-woman play, Clara Bow, *has, as of this writing, yet to be presented on a stage, it has been performed on audio by Nancy McLemore and that production is available on Amazon, audio.com and iTunes.*

Interestingly, the paperback and Kindle editions of Clara Bow *are, by far, the best selling of all the plays in* The Hollywood Legends *collection. I've been told that drama students often present scenes from the play as classroom projects.*

The play was written in 1985. In researching it, I visited with Charles "Buddy" Rogers, Clara's co-star in Wings, *and I also flew to Las Vegas to spend a day with her son, Rex Bell, Jr., who worked with the district attorney's office.*

I also recall a telephone conversation with actor Gilbert Roland, but, sadly, those interview notes seem to have disappeared.

Charles "Buddy" Rogers

"Clara was always vivacious; like bubbling champagne."

"We had a wild time in San Antonio when we shot *Wings*. We took over the whole hotel. It was one big party."

"Clara was always trying to please everyone."

Rex Bell, Jr.

"Mom loved watching football. She'd bet on the throws."

"Father Bow was a tyrant. He was known as "King Bow."

"He was a 'stage father'. He pushed every aspect of Mom's life that he could, but he couldn't get by Rex.[1]

"My grandfather was a bigot; hated Jews. Clara would have married Gilbert Roland, except her father hated Mexicans."

"I learned discipline from my mother. If my clothes weren't hung up and neat when I went to bed, she'd wake me up and make me take care of them"

"Mother taught me to swim by throwing me into the pool."

1 Rex Bell, Sr. had been a "B" picture cowboy star when he met and married Clara. Later, he was elected Lieutenant Governor of Nevada.

"Mom said that Gary Cooper[2] was completely controlled by his mother."

"Ego was always a problem in my parents' marriage. In one way or another, Mom let Rex know that she was 'great'. She lorded her acting success over him. It hurt his feelings."

"We were a family of tigers. We loved one another, but didn't display affection. We were independent. We each played our own game."

"My parents' lifestyles ran out. She had insomnia and retreated from the world. She wouldn't go out and Dad couldn't stay up with her."

"Even after they separated, my parents would spend every Christmas with each other in Los Angeles. They still loved each other"

2 Clara and Cooper had a long term affair.

Orson Welles

Orson Welles

Orson Welles has fascinated me ever since I first saw Citizen Kane during my years at the University of Washington. Indeed, one of my term papers was devoted to the actor/director's work.

I never met the man, which is probably just as well, because based on everything I know about him, we would probably not have liked each other. The closest I ever got to him was chatting with his early collaborator, John Houseman, at a party and my long friendship with actor Dan O'Herlihy, who played "MacDuff" in Welles' filming of Shakespeare's Macbeth.

I wrote my one-person play, Orson Welles, in 1986, and it was first presented at the Center Stage Theater in Woodland, Hills, California on October 22, 1992, with Art Kempf playing Welles.

Subsequently, the play has had a couple of productions in other parts of the country, but it has also been produced on audio with Edward French doing the role. That production is available for download via Amazon, audio.com and iTunes.

In researching this play, I interviewed film critic Arthur Knight and actor Dan O'Herlihy.

Arthur Knight

"He was a charming man. He showed interest in the other person. He called me at home one night to praise a book I'd written. He made you feel you were equally important.

"Orson liked to talk. One subject would just lead to another."

Actor Dan O'Herlihy and the author

Dan O'Herlihy

"He had charm, charisma; a sense of power.

"Orson played power."

"It had been years since I'd seen Orson when we did *Waterloo* (1970) together.

"The last time I'd seen him, he had started to put on weight, and he said to me: 'I'm going to give up chocolate.'

"I went over to his dressing room, and there he was, sitting in front of the mirror, his back to me. He was enormous.

"I stood in the doorway, and after a moment, he saw me standing behind him in the mirror.

He smiled, and I said: 'I see you've given up chocolate.'"

The Unforgotten Photo

On my 76th birthday, my son, David, sent me a terrific gift. He discovered it while going through a box of his late mother's things.

It was a photo of me and actor Sal Mineo (*Rebel Without a Cause, Exodus*).

I hadn't seen this photo for close to forty years. Indeed, I thought it was lost. Otherwise, I would have included it in my first memoir, *My Forty-Five Years in Hollywood... And How I Escaped Alive,* in which I wrote about my dealings with Sal.

The picture was taken in 1966 at The Playboy Club in Los Angeles. Sal and I were discussing a film project that he'd hired me to write for him. We wrote a treatment of the script, but the project never went further than that. I did get paid, and Sal and I remained friendly until his tragic death in 1976.

This photo could become a collector's item. It's one of the few pictures you'll see of me sans beard.

The author with actor Sal Mineo

Some Final Words

The Hollywood that I loved and wanted to be a part of no longer exists.

Perhaps it never really did.

It was an illusion.

But, it was a wonderful illusion, masterfully created by the motion picture studios in order to sell their wares.

It inspired people with a creative bent to dream and to follow their dreams to Hollywood.

Most of those dreamers would fall by the wayside, their flights of imagination shattered. A very few would achieve incredible success, while the rest of those romantics who "shot for the stars" found themselves "in the treetops" and realized that the treetops were the best place to be after all.

I enjoy living in the treetops. It's comfortable here.

It was technology and business interests that finally destroyed any semblance of the Hollywood illusion. In the beginning, there was just live theatre, movies and radio. Then, television, with its mere thirteen channels, came along. Then, came cable TV, home video, and now, streaming.

On cable alone, there are hundreds of entertainment choices vying for your attention. Who has time to even consider watching but a mere handful?

It's no secret that entertainment has always been a business, but in the past, studio heads looked to the future. They created stars and those stars became financial assets.

Yes, the motion picture studios are still around, but they no longer develop stars who can draw an audience, let alone become legendary. They just sell product these days. If a star is in their film or television series, the studio or network will promote him. If not, that performer is on his own.

Indeed, I don't believe that there is one actor or actress today whose name can guarantee the success of a movie or a television program. Audiences are spread too thin.

Today, the movie or the television show is "the star," not the actor or actress. A name performer can certainly enhance and draw initial interest to a project, but they cannot save it if the audience refuses to embrace it.

The show business waters got muddied even more a few years back when hi-def video cameras came onto the market.

The *good* news was that, with this new device, anybody could make a movie.

The *bad* news was that, with this new device, anybody could make a movie.

Dreamers with a few bucks, borrowed or otherwise, and virtually no practical experience in filmmaking, began producing feature films that nobody, with the possible exception of family and *very* close friends, wanted to see. The finished products were either ineptly made or, if they were somewhat professionally done and had some entertainment value, lacked a viable marketing hook (e.g. a star, intriguing storyline).[1]

In the past, a movie that could not get a theatrical release, might wind up on television or cable, which always seems to need product. Failing that, it could go direct to home video release,[2] but that market has pretty much faded in favor of streaming.

So, what does a filmmaker do with his unwanted movie today?

Well, there's always YouTube, or there are some websites that charge viewers a monthly/annual subscription fee (or a dollar or two) to download

---

1 *Paranormal Activity* (2007) is one of a very few notable exceptions. The production cost was $15,000. The picture was sold to Paramount for $350,000, and the movie grossed $193 million worldwide.

2 Even major stars like Marlon Brando were not immune to that fate. His 1998 film, *Free Money*, was released direct to home video in the USA.

their unknown movies. But, then again, who but family or very close friends would be interested?

Ironically, the majority of the films that win awards these days are *not* studio films. They were conceived and, for the most part, produced by independents. True, a studio might have supplied some later financing and distribution, but these projects, unlike in decades past, did not begin with them. Studios, it seems, are primarily interested in producing blockbusters (e.g. *Batman v Superman: Dawn of Justice*).

I have no idea where the entertainment industry will be in the next decade or two. I'm not the only one who believes that the movie theater/multiplex, as we know it, will disappear. Certainly making a film available for streaming the same day it's released into theaters accelerates this process.

There may be movie theaters, but they will only be used for gigantic special productions that would not play well in a smaller venue. With audiences being able to view everything from *Ben-Hur* to *Avatar* on their iPads or cell phones, who needs to pay the high admission fees in order to sit in a crowded theater to see your average movie?

Unlike Jack Warner, Louis B. Mayer, Harry Cohn and the other studio moguls of days gone by, all of who seemed to have an innate sense of what their audiences wanted to see,[3] today's studio heads rely on committees and "scientific" polls in deciding what movies and television shows will go before the camera.

Also, the advent of CGI has certainly allowed filmmakers to take their audiences into thrilling worlds that were not available prior to that computer art form. Sadly, in so many pictures today, those CGI wonders have replaced good storytelling.

Growing up in 1950s Seattle, I recall that movies like *Roman Holiday* or *Sabrina*, both starring Audrey Hepburn, would play in one downtown the-

---

3 He may be an independent producer, but my former boss, Roger Corman, also has that innate sense of what *his* audience wants to see.

ater for over a year before it moved out into the neighborhood houses. Audience word-of-mouth created a "want to see" factor for these and other films.

However, since the advent of *Jaws* in the 1970s, most studio movies open in multiple houses nation- and city-wide, and if they don't do well that first week, the studio virtually abandons them and they are written off as a loss.

It used to be that it took years before a theatrical movie, particularly a successful one, played on television. Today, studios are more interested in squeezing as much money out of a picture as quickly as possible. That's why, within a very few months after its theatrical release, you can rent a movie at RedBox and/or stream it into your home.[4] Shortly thereafter, that film is available to HBO or Showtime subscribers, and within a year or two, free television.

Unfortunately, greed in the motion picture industry has replaced showmanship.

But, I rant too much. So, let's just say this:

The "Golden Age of Hollywood," such as it was, exists only in our memories. Even so, I do miss it.

4 I have not been inside a movie theater for over three years. If there is a film that I *really* want to see, I wait the 2-3 months and rent it from RedBox for $1.60.

About the Author

Michael B. Druxman is a veteran Hollywood screenwriter whose credits include *Cheyenne Warrior* with Kelly Preston; *Dillinger and Capone* starring Martin Sheen and F. Murray Abraham; and *The Doorway* with Roy Scheider, which he also directed.

He is also a prolific playwright, his one-person play, *Jolson,* having had numerous productions around the country. Other produced stage credits include one-person plays about Clark Gable, Carole Lombard, Spencer Tracy and Orson Welles. These and plays about Errol Flynn, Maurice Chevalier, Clara Bow, Basil Rathbone and Jeanette MacDonald and Nelson Eddy, as well as *B Movie,* a three-character play that deals with the sordid 1950s sex scandal involving actors Franchot Tone, Barbara Payton and Tom Neal, *Sexy Rexy,* a five character play about Rex Harrison and the women in his life, and *Lana & Johnny Were Lovers,* a four character play about the Lana Turner/ Johnny Stompanato affair, have been individually published under the collective title of *The Hollywood Legends.*

His most recent contributions to *The Hollywood Legends* collection are *Robinson & Raft,* a three-character play dealing with movie tough guys Edward G. Robinson and George Raft, *The Last Monsters,* a five-character play featuring horror icons Lon Chaney, Jr., Bela Lugosi and John Carradine, and *Ava & Her Guys,* populated by Ava Gardner, Mickey Rooney, Artie Shaw and Frank Sinatra .

Additionally, Mr. Druxman is the author of more than fifteen published books, including several nonfiction works about Hollywood, its movies, and the people who make them (e.g., *Paul Muni: His Life and His Films, Basil Rathbone: His Life and His Films, Make It Again, Sam: A Survey of Movie Remakes, One Good Film Deserves Another: A Survey of Movie Sequels, Charlton Heston, Merv* [Griffin], *The Musical: From Broadway to Hollywood*) and *Miss Dinah Shore.*

He has written three novels, *Nobody Drowns in Mineral Lake, Shadow Watcher* and *Murder in Babylon,* a book of short stories, entitled *Dracula Meets Jack the Ripper & Other Revisionist Histories,* plus the humorous revisionist history, *Once Upon a Time in Hollywood: From the Secret Files of Harry Pennypacker,* and *Family Secret,* a non-fiction book co-authored with Warren Hull, which reveals the true facts behind the 1947 murder of mobster "Bugsy" Siegel in Beverly Hills.

An acknowledged Hollywood historian, he has also written television documentaries and has been interviewed for various retrospective featurettes that have accompanied DVD releases of classic films (e.g. *The Maltese Falcon, The Hound of the Baskervilles,* etc.).

Mr. Druxman is a former Hollywood publicist of 35 years experience who has represented many film and television stars, as well as noted directors, producers and composers. One of his Academy Award campaigns is often mentioned in books dealing with Oscar's history.

He has taught various dramatic writing and film appreciation courses in an adult university and is the author of *How to Write a Story... Any Story: The Art of Storytelling,* which has been used as a text in several colleges. He is often invited to speak to groups of aspiring film and television professionals to discuss screenwriting and the realities of show business.

A native of Seattle who graduated from Garfield High School and the University of Washington, Mr. Druxman moved with his wife, Sandy, from Los Angeles to Austin, TX in 2009.

His memoirs, *My Forty-Five Years in Hollywood and How I Escaped Alive* (2010) and *Life, Liberty & The Pursuit of Hollywood* (2013) are published by Bear Manor Media.